With Good Intentions?

WITH GOOD INTENTIONS?

Reflections on the Myth of Progress in America

BILL KAUFFMAN

Westport, Connecticut
London

Library of Congress Cataloging-in-Publication Data

Kauffman, Bill, 1959–
   With good intentions? : reflections on the myth of progress in
America / Bill Kauffman.
      p. cm.
   Includes bibliographical references and index.
   ISBN 0–275–96270–9 (alk. paper)
   1. Dissenters—United States.   2. Progressivism (United States
politics) I. Title.
HN57.K365   1998
303.48′4—dc21   98–11125

British Library Cataloguing in Publication Data is available.

Library of Congress Catalog Card Number: 98–11125
ISBN: 0–275–96270–9

First published in 1998

Praeger Publishers, 88 Post Road West, Westport, CT 06881
An imprint of Greenwood Publishing Group, Inc.

Printed in the United States of America

(∞)™

The paper used in this book complies with the
Permanent Paper Standard issued by the National
Information Standards Organization (Z39.48–1984).

10 9 8 7 6 5 4 3 2 1

Copyright Acknowledgments

The author and the publisher are grateful to the following sources for granting permission
to reprint from their materials:

Excerpts from THE WALLACES OF IOWA. Copyright © 1947, renewed 1975 by Russell
Lord. Reprinted by permission of Houghton Mifflin Company. All rights reserved.

Excerpts reprinted by permission of Louisiana State University Press from *I'll Take My
Stand: The South and the Agrarian Tradition*, by Twelve Southerners; New Introduction
by Louis D. Rubin, Jr. Copyright © 1930 by Harper & Brothers. Copyright © renewed 1958
by Donald Davidson. Introduction copyright © 1962, 1977 by Louis D. Rubin, Jr. Biographi-
cal essays copyright © 1962, 1977 by Virginia Rock. Louisiana State University Press.

For Jane, who gave me paper and pencils.

Contents

Preface

The western New York village of Le Roy—pronounced La-Roy, vaguely regal, by its residents; and Leee-Roy, as in Jordan or Selmon, by the rest of us—is a goldmine of nicknames. Its leafy streets have been populated by Pickle, Boomer, Weegie, and, my favorite, the late great "Eggs" Bacon.

But a fissure has developed. The Interstate Highway System, that human conveyor belt and model of government-subsidized mobility, opened a Le Roy exchange several years ago, and Rochester yuppies who didn't mind a half-hour commute could purchase their own little half-acres of quaintness. An unpalatable cleft resulted, and nowhere is this more evident than in the use of sobriquets. Old-time Le Royans (including several relatives of mine) still traffic in nicknames, but the newer folk, for the most part, do not. It's not that they don't want charming monikers hung 'round their necks; it's just that they haven't *earned* them. For most nicknames attach themselves in childhood and are not portable: abandon the scene of your boyhood and bid farewell to Tiny Tim.

To acquire a nickname is easy; to maintain one is harder, as it requires continuous residence in one place. The Interstate has disrupted local patterns of commerce and life; in Le Roy, a small—but ultimately significant—casualty has been nicknames.

Even the harshest critics of modernity tend to regard such losses as unavoidable. Urbanization, the disappearance of rural "district" schools, the transfer of production from the home to the factory, the K-Mart/Wal-Mart vanquishment of locally owned shops, the intrusion of the state and its agents across the hearthstone, the militarization of American life and economy: these are occasionally lamented, but wistfully so, as with the passing of vivid autumn into gray winter. Whether progress is a matter of triste or treat, all concede its inevitability.

"You can't turn back the clock," expostulate those who mistake weariness for wisdom. Yet these believers in history, foreordained, never seem to consider the possibility that their watches show the wrong time.

This book examines—sympathetically—the people, movements, and arguments of six hopelessly (or so it might seem) "lost causes": opposition to school consolidation, the Interstate Highway System, woman suffrage, and the maintenance of a large standing army; and the defense of child labor and the back-to-the-land movement of the Great Depression.

A forlorn sextet? As any Le Royan could tell you, her schools are consolidated, her father and uncles were conscripted or paid to travel far from home in the armed services, in her girlhood she was forbidden to work for more than a few carefully regulated hours, she can vote for the president of the United States (though she probably does so without enthusiasm), her village is connected with the big city of Rochester via two Interstate routes, and, unless she is one of the dwindling number of farmers who own most of the arable land in Genesee County, she is not one of nature's noblewomen.

Do I curse the wind for blowing or the sun for setting? No. For each and every one of these putatively "inevitable" sea changes in American life was the result of noncontroversial (for the most part), sometimes virtually uncontested government policy. At the time, it seemed that all people of goodwill agreed that: the one-room schoolhouse was obsolete; children should be in school, not working on the family farm; women should have the vote; agrarianism is impractical in an industrial society; our highway system has connected the disparate parts of a nation and helped us to prosper; the military cultivates virtues.

Yet the consequences of these axioms have been, in some cases, devastating. Our citizens have been uprooted. Authentic communities have weakened while the central state has battened. Families have been subordinated to the therapists and credentialed experts who would deny us even the sheerest loincloth of privacy. People of goodwill ofttimes make bad policy.

In one sense the chapter on the antisuffragists—or "Antis"—is anomalous, for I regard woman suffrage, unlike consolidation and empire and the rest, to have been a just and beneficial reform. But the Antis, as will be shown, were no self-abnegating shawl-covered church mice—unless Emma Goldman and Ida Tarbell are to be regarded as such. They were, rather, part of the antiprogressive (or anti-Progress, with a capital P, since to call "Halt!" to the long march is an act of heresy) tradition illuminated in this book.

The anti-Progress dissidents discussed herein were by and large Jeffersonians. Faithful to the old Republic, motivated by agrarian biases even when they lived in cities, their bedrocks were (1) family autonomy; (2) a minimal state; and (3) human-scale communities.

The Antis, as with the other recusants, argued that seemingly unassailable reforms that promised greater liberty, greater happiness, and greater prosperity, would in fact constrict liberty and alter social relations and civic life in such a way that we would become estranged from each other and the community and dependent upon the impersonal state. (See, in chapter 3, the argument between Anti Ida Tarbell and suffrage leader Anna Howard Shaw over women and the Beef Trust. Down Miss Shaw's way lies Wal-Mart.)

Throughout the book I have made literary men and women, American novelists and poets, from John Greenleaf Whittier to Sinclair Lewis, a kind of anti-Progress chorus. They knew, if the politicians did not, that mobility deranges character; that deracination drains our souls; that sequacity toward the state is both enfeebling and un-American. This is not to say, of course, that no highways should ever be built, any more than it is to say that women should not have gotten the vote. But there is a cost—often hidden, unacknowledged—to these advances, and though my own preference is for woman suffrage and against the Interstate Highway System, the anti-Progress critique can encompass both—and can introduce us to a valuable way of thinking about and reckoning change, even if we judge the change to be for the best.

The Antis, the Jeffersonian agrarians, the decentralists who stood their ground in the eye of the hurricane, were both reactionary and radical. They were reactionary in their hostility to state action and state-directed dynamism, and in their idealization of an earlier, family-based, virtually stateless political and social order; radical in their refusal to accept a fate engineered by others. They people our forgotten history. Most have gotten a bad historiographical press—when they are mentioned at all. Yet these skeptics of the great god Progress have much to teach us, even when they may have been wrong on particulars.

As for Le Roy—the old still have nicknames, as do those young people who, through inertia or dedication, stayed home. (Consider a pair of colloquialisms. "He'll go far," approving elders say of promising youngsters, with the implication that success can be measured in the distance one has traveled from home. If, on the other hand, we say of a boy, "He's not going anywhere," we are not praising his steadfastness but damning him as an ambitionless sluggard. Absence may make the heart grow fonder, but love's greatest demand is immobility.)

Le Roy's central school, which swelled in the 1940s as smaller district schools were closed and consolidated, is under pressure from outsiders and the state bureaucracy to merge with the school in Pavilion, a very different town several miles down the road. Faithful Le Royans have resisted the urge to merge (and be submerged), but the consolidationists are biding their time until a critical mass of the citizenry is composed of commuters and bedroom residents. Then Le Roy—or the pod that will go by the name Le Roy, à la *Invasion of the Body Snatchers*—can become ever less itself and ever less a place worthy of its ancestors. But more on school consolidation in chapter 2.

In Booth Tarkington's novel *The Turmoil* (1915), Bibbs Sheridan, dreamy son of an industrialist, asks, "Wasn't the whole country happier and in many ways wiser when it was smaller and cleaner and quieter and kinder?"

The obscure men and women we shall meet in the following pages thought so. And their work, their writings, their very lives, tell us that it didn't have to be this way.

Acknowledgments

I am grateful to editors and publishers Chris Check, Allan Carlson, Karl Zinsmeister, and Lew Rockwell for the opportunity to try out earlier versions of some chapters and paragraphs in their journals. Chris stuck his neck out for me: I owe him thanks and admiration. And I thank the Liberty Fund for sponsoring my work on the Child Labor Amendment.

I am blessed beyond measure with a home, a place, a family. Lucine and Gretel, my parents and relatives, my town and friends, teach me every day the beauty of the lost beatitude: Blessed are those who stay put.

With Good Intentions?

1

Catholics and Mugwumps and Farmers: The Debate over Child Labor

> No fledgling feeds the father bird,
>   No chicken feeds the hen—
> No kitten mouses for the cat,
>   This glory is for men.
> We are the Wisest, Strongest Race—
>   Loud may our praise be sung!
> The only animal alive
>   That lives upon its young.
>
> —Charlotte Perkins Gilman[1]

Here you are, a Jeffersonian Democrat, the cardinal principle of which doctrine was the integrity of the states, urging me, a Hamiltonian Republican, to support a constitutional amendment enabling the national government to deal with the children of the states. Strange times, these are. But I think I can encourage you to expect favorable action, as the women always get nowadays what they ask for.

> —Senator William Borah (R-ID) to a constituent, 1924[2]

. . . a communistic effort to nationalize children, making them primarily responsible to the government instead of to their parents. It strikes at the home. It appears to be a definite positive plan to destroy the Republic and substitute a social democracy.

> —Clarence E. Martin
> President, American Bar Association[3]

When the right of a father to govern his own family is taken away from him, God pity our Nation.

> —D. H. Petree
> Florida legislator[4]

The movement to regulate child labor began as a New England parlor revolt against industrialism, or at least its grimier, more noisome aspects. Gradually, well-intentioned reformers with modest goals gave way to socialists whose reconstructionist dreams included the interposition of the state between the parent and the child.

The "gaunt goblin army"[5] of teenaged workers was cashiered by a series of laws prohibiting employment and prescribing schooling. Mission, ostensibly, accomplished. But the triumph was incomplete: the child labor amendment to the Constitution was rejected. Thwarted were what Columbia University president Nicholas Murray Butler called "more far-reaching . . . changes in our family, social, economic, and political life than have heretofore been dreamed of by the most ardent revolutionary."[6]

Nascent American industries frequently employed families of the working class. Alexander Hamilton had remarked, in his "Report on Manufactures," that "children are rendered more useful . . . by manufacturing establishments than they would otherwise be."[7]

As the mill towns grew, so did the conviction of many genteel ladies that boys and girls ought to be scholars, not mill doffers. Ella Wheeler Wilcox keened:

> In this boasted land of freedom there are bonded baby slaves,
> And the busy world goes by and does not heed.
> They are driven to the mill, just to glut and overfill
> Bursting coffers of the mighty monarch, Greed.
> When they perish we are told it is God's will,
> Oh, the roaring of the mill, of the mill![8]

Contrasting views of child labor are found in the novels of Horatio Alger and the Gilded Age fictions of a passel of New England women novelists.

Alger did not neglect the vice and dirt that spattered the forlorn "Child of the Street," but his glasses were tinted roseate. Tatterdemalion boys full of pluck and guile acted out the Algerian philosophy that "in the boot-blacking business, as well as in higher avocations, the same rule prevails, that energy and industry are rewarded, and indolence suffers."[9] Labor neither ennobles nor degrades the poor boy; it is simply necessary to his advancement. (Alger hero Ragged Dick Hunter was not immune to the depraving influences of the street. His newsboy career ended when he sold out his *New York Herald*s with the pitch, "Queen Victoria Assassinated!")

There were no indomitable Ragged Dicks in Elizabeth Stuart Phelps's influential 1871 novel, *The Silent Partner*. Phelps's heroine, the righteous spinster Perley Kelso, is the daughter of a Massachusetts mill owner. Upon learning that "factory girls ate black molasses and had the cotton-cough,"[10] Perley undertakes the reformation of the Five Falls working class. Weekly teas are inaugurated, at which mill hands mix with proper Boston girls; the beaux arts are cultivated; pacified and uplifted, the workers cheerfully accept a pay cut.

The Silent Partner is a charmingly naive piece of didacticism by a woman whom Vernon Parrington called "an Andover Brahmin, highly sensitive, whose deeply religious nature was ruffled by every vagrant wind."[11] Perley Kelso presaged a new generation of reforming women for whom the home—the working class home, at least—was no longer the inviolable castle defined by William Pitt: "The poorest man may, in his cottage, bid defiance to all the force of the Crown. It may be frail—the roof may shake; the wind may blow through it; the storms may enter; the rain may enter—but the King of England can not enter; all his forces may not cross the threshold of the ruined tenement."[12]

After Perley meets the eight-year-old urchin Bub Mell, a billingsgate-spewing mill boy and marble-sharp, she barges into Mell pere's apartment and confronts the feckless dad:

He was out so late about the streets, Mr. Mell. He uses tobacco as most children use candy. And a child of that age ought not to be in the mills, sir, he ought to be at school!. . . The stairs in this house are in shocking condition. What is—excuse me—the very peculiar odor which I notice on these premises?[13]

Poor Mell's ruined tenement launches Perley on a life of good works. She never will marry; reform is her spouse. The Mell threshold offers as little resistance to her as a turnstile. Years later, the *Woman Patriot* would note of the schemes of Perley's living breathing counterparts: "It is solely the poor man's right of castle that is sacrificed."[14]

How many Ragged Dicks and Bub Mells were there? The federal census reported that in 1880, 1.18 million children between the ages of ten and fifteen (16.8% of all such children) were "gainfully employed." In 1890 that number climbed to 1.75 million (18.2%) and in 1910, 1.99 million (18.4%).

But these two million were hardly a gaunt goblin army: Census-takers enumerated those farm children who constituted a "material addition" to the family income. Plowboys and farmers' daughters far outnumbered young cannery and coal-mine workers. Of the two million child laborers counted in the 1910 census, 72 percent were farm kids, about 85 percent of whom worked on the family acres.

Farm labor, admittedly exhausting, was at first unassailable by the Perley Kelsos. Outdoor chores were salubrious, offering "none of the hazards of mines and factories to the growing body and soul."[15] Novelist Hamlin Garland, no dreamy pastoralist, wrote:

There are certain ameliorations to child labor on a farm. Air and sunshine and food are plentiful. I never lacked for meat or clothing, and mingled with my records of toil are exquisite memories of the joy I took in following the changes in the landscape, in the notes of birds, and in the play of small animals on the sunny soil.[16]

Moreover, farm children worked under the direction of their parents. They ate and wore the fruits of their labor, inspiring Jefferson's comment that "every family in the country is a manufactory within itself, and is very generally able to make within itself all the stouter and middling stuffs for its own clothing and household use."[17]

So Hamilton's useful drudges in the factories, mills, and mines were the first candidates for deliverance. Next would be the tens of thousands of Ragged Dicks plying the street trades on city sidewalks. The farms were as yet off-limits—awaiting a Progressive moment.

It all began in New England. In 1836, Massachusetts barred children under fifteen from jobs in manufacturing unless they had attended school for at least three of the preceding twelve months. (The best child-labor law is compulsory schooling, went the maxim.) Six years later, the Bay State forbade children under twelve from working more than ten hours a day; by midcentury, every state in the region had similar restrictions. By century's end, twenty-eight states had enacted child-labor laws, usually setting a minimum age (fourteen for factory work), prohibiting night work, and requiring school attendance.

In 1872, the Prohibitionists became the first party to nail a child-labor plank into their platform. (Half a century later, Child Labor Amendment foes would be arraigned as wets, reactionary kid-abusing sots.) The cause attracted dozens of Democratic and Republican paladins, though the parties did not formally endorse federal legislation until 1912, when a bidding war erupted for the votes of Progressives.

This "crusade for the children," as its adult warriors dubbed it, bogged down in the South. Parents, many of them new in the mill towns, just in from the piedmont or the hardscrabble, "felt the children should continue to do their part to help support the family, just as they had done on the farm."[18]

Sectional enmity flared. The reformers, largely of Northeastern mint, were seen as meddling do-gooders at best, agents of New England mills at worst. David Clark, the pugnacious editor of the *Southern Textile Bulletin*, claimed (without adducing much evidence) that the crusade "was financed to a considerable extent by New England cotton manufacturers in order to reduce competition."[19] (In 1900, only 10% of minors employed in industry were of the South; natheless, the region came to be associated with this social blight. The actual number of non-agricultural child laborers was higher in Pennsylvania than in all Confederate states combined.)

Even Southern proponents of child-labor laws resented outside interference. Populist South Carolina Senator "Pitchfork" Ben Tillman, a charter member of the National Child Labor Committee, railed against "Northern millionaires who have gone down there and built mills and made industrial slaves out of white children instead of the chattel black slaves of the old days."[20] (Yankee activists also spoke ominously of the "race degeneracy and race suicide"[21] committed when white tykes toddled off to the mills while black kids went to school.)

Episcopal clergyman Edgar Gardner Murphy, a son of Fort Smith, Arkansas, who was trained at Columbia University and the General Theological Seminary, emerged as the movement's Southern knight. Murphy, though no agrarian—"the cotton mills," he wrote, "indeed our factories of every sort, are bringing their blessings to the South"[22]—lamented the ruin of derusticated families. Fathers, indispensable on the farm, were less so in the factory. The idle papa, lazing and drinking while mama and junior toiled the livelong day, became an object of obloquy. "Back of nearly every child at work," steamed Miss Jean M. Gordon, factory inspector of Louisiana, "is a lazy, shiftless father or an incompetent mother."[23]

The mills tore at the family in other ways. Murphy explained:

> Upon the farm the child labors, as it labors in the home, under the eye of a guardianship which is usually that of the parent, which is full of a parental solicitude. . . . In the factory the child works as an industrial unit, a little member of an industrial aggregate, under an oversight which must, of necessity, be administrative rather than personal.[24]

At Murphy's prodding, in 1903 his adopted state of Alabama forbade children under twelve from working in factories—the strictest standard in the South. By decade's end, every state legislature in the South, save that of Georgia, had passed a minimum-age law. (Oglethorpe's commonwealth did punish able-bodied fathers who lived off the labor of their progeny.)

Murphy's abilities—and his Southern pedigree—won him a following in New York City. He and Felix Adler founded the National Child Labor Committee on April 15, 1904 at Carnegie Hall. The NCLC was small but puissant; its directorate read like a *Who's Who* of plutocrats and uplifters, virtually all resident in New York City and its overspill: John D. Rockefeller, E. H. Harriman, J. P. Morgan, Paul Warburg, Andrew Carnegie, Adolph C. Ochs, Gifford Pinchot, and a flock of "idle-rich, sentimental, good-hearted women."[25] Southern cousins included future Georgia governor Hoke Smith and the aforementioned firebrand, Tillman.

Tillman excepted, the NCLC and kindred organizations had no luck recruiting Populists and other agrarian radicals. Paternalism ran counter to the Populist character. Says Casy, the itinerant preacher in John Steinbeck's *The Grapes of Wrath*: "On'y one thing in this worl' I'm sure of, an' that's I'm sure nobody got a right to mess with a fella's life. He got to do it all hisself. Help him, maybe, but not tell him what to do."[26]

The NCLC lobbied state legislatures to: set minimum ages of fourteen in manufactures and sixteen in mining; limit children to an eight-hour day; and ban work after 7:00 P.M. The southern cotton mills, and the Pennsylvania coal mines, where "breaker boys" picked slate and slag from the black chutes, coastal canneries, and urban street trades, were the NCLC's prime targets.

The newsboy's life, so picturesque, came in for special condemnation. Sing Sing warden Lewis E. Lawes testified that 69 percent of his inmates had hawked dailies.[27] Profanity, gambling, fast women, even "the dubious frankfurter"[28] conspired to corrupt the Ragged Dicks of the pavement. Messenger boys faced even greater temptations: polemicist John Spargo despaired, "Sad to relate, boys like to be employed in 'red-light' districts."[29]

Alger notwithstanding, few Ragged Dicks were orphans. NCLC operative E. C. Clopper found that over 75 percent of four hundred Cincinnati newsboys were from intact families. Myron E. Adams, a New York City social worker, determined that "only a very small number" of boys in the street trades were from alms-deserving families. Josephine Goldmark reported that just one-quarter of the incarcerated ex-newsboys she studied were raised by widows.[30] The point that Clopper et al. wanted to make was that the labor of children was not necessary to the economic life of the family; dad's wages (and maybe mom's, too) were sufficient. Inadvertently, they painted a picture of the newsboy as the product of a solid home.

The battle shifted to Washington after a marathon three-day speech in January 1907 by Senator Albert Beveridge (R-IN), an apostle of Teddy Roosevelt progressivism. Beveridge's address was filled with fantastic allegations, though none dared call them mendacious. Relying on the notarized depositions of socialists Scott Nearing, Florence Kelley, and John Spargo, Beveridge narrated lurid tales of thumbless boys and girls who "don't know how to play."[31] He concluded, "More than a million children are dying of overwork or being forever stunted and dwarfed in body, mind, and soul."[32]

Child labor was an evil to be extirpated, in the same way that lotteries and obscene literature had been forever banished from God's republic: by federal law. (In a colloquy with Senator Tillman, Beveridge volunteered, "I have no objection to the working of children in the open air; . . . labor on a farm within their strength is a good thing."[33] But once out of the gate, the hobbyhorse outgalloped the senator.)

Beveridge proposed to prohibit the interstate transportation of articles produced in factories or mines that employed children under age fourteen. His bill rent the NCLC asunder. Its New York City–dominated board endorsed it, prompting Edgar Gardner Murphy, a principled states-rights man, to resign. (Unwilling to let its prize southerner slip away, the NCLC rescinded its support of federal action, at least until Reverend Murphy died in 1913.)[34]

Once into the drink, the Beveridge bill began its long upstream swim. Meanwhile, a Federal Children's Bureau was created within the Department of Commerce and Labor.[35] This information-gathering agency, invaluable in the coming propaganda war, boasted a payroll reading like Hull House East.

The bureau bill's supporters professed its innocuousness. We already gather data on the "diseases of hogs and cattle and sheep,"[36] they reasoned; aren't kids at least as important? Opponents harped on the threat that the bureau's investigators might pose to the poor man's right of castle. "The unmarried of the country who know how to raise children"[37] will be loosed upon "the class that is most helpless in their hands—those who toil for a living,"[38] warned Senator Weldon Heyburn (R-ID). Why, these uplifters would've

taken Abraham Lincoln from his parents' care. . . . Some committee . . . would have gone down there and said, "What, allow that child to lie down there and eat corn pone and hoecake by the hearth; he can not possibly amount to anything; we want to take him down to the headquarters, where we are drawing salaries for taking care of that kind of people."[39]

By a 39 to 34 vote, Heyburn and Senator Charles A. Culberson (D-TX) added a right-of-castle amendment to the bill: "No official or representative of said bureau shall, over the objection of the head of the family, enter any . . . family residence."[40] Notice had been served; there were limits beyond which the child-savers could not go. Thus amended, the bureau bill passed, 54 to 20; President William H. Taft signed it into law on April 9, 1912. Hull Houser Julia Lathrop was appointed to head the Children's Bureau, with a modest budget of $25,000 at her disposal.

Defenders of child labor in the mills and factories at first favored paternalistic arguments. Thomas Dawley, Jr., a disgruntled government inspector of southern mills, indicted the muckrakers for "misrepresentations so gross . . . as fairly to astound an unbiased mind."[41] Sent to Asheville, North Carolina, Dawley looked up that city's two most prominent children's crusaders: a minister and a social worker newly arrived from New York City—neither of whom had ever been inside a cotton mill. When Dawley entered, he found "bright, vivacious"[42] mill girls and "happy and contented"[43] boys, working none too hard and learning in mill-built schools. Contrasted with the "mountain homes of squalor"[44] Dawley had seen, the mills were godsends. A Tennessee innkeeper told Dawley, "Why, thar' ain't enough cotton-mills to take care o' them poor chil'ren what's in our mountains. If thar' only war . . . it would be the greates' thing in the world fer 'em."[45]

Apologists played up the advantages of living in a company town: steady wages, nearby churches and schools and libraries, public parks . . . indeed, civilization.[46] The sweat and toil of children was said to be indispensable. Lewis B. Parker, a Greenville, South Carolina, cotton manufacturer, explained, "All the people who are poverty stricken or who can not make a success of anything else have gravitated to the cotton mills." The pool of skilled adult labor was yet too small: "We can not possibly [move] from . . . agriculturalism to . . . industrialism without the employment of minors."[47]

Julia Magruder, replying in the *North American Review* to "ignorant sentimentalists"[48] who bled sugar over the two million scurvy-wretched baby slaves, claimed: "The class from which the millhands in the South are drawn is the very lowest . . . [Praise be] the elevating and civilizing influence of the cotton-mills."[49]

Hadn't New England long demanded the mental and spiritual maturation of poor southern whites? Ralph Waldo Emerson was willing to accept worse cotton if it meant better men; well, said the industrialists, the mill towns were improving both.

Mill families themselves were downright hostile to the prohibitionists. (As if the opinions of poor whites have ever really mattered.) "Some of the most devoted advocates of child labor . . . were the young themselves and their own parents,"[50] noted one labor historian. Southern parents, to the bitter dismay of reformers, evaded the laws by lying about the ages of their offspring.

Northerners were no less obdurate. Inconveniently for the NCLC, child laborers were neither mute nor idiot; many resented their benefactresses. Inspector Helen Todd asked five hundred children in twenty Chicago factories, "If your father had a good job, and you didn't have to work, which would you rather do—go to school or work in a factory?" To Miss Todd's horror, 412 chose the factory.[51]

Looking back, many adults no doubt rue spending their nonage at hard labor. Bertha Awford Black, after a lifetime in the Amazon Mills in Thomasville, North Carolina, recalled:

> We'd go out there behind the mill at the warehouse and us girls we'd build us a little playhouse until they'd whistle for us and yell, "Time for the doffers to piece up again." Just nothing but children. You know, that ought to have been stopped a long time before it was. We didn't get no education. We weren't old enough to go to work. That thar child labor law was wonderful when it came in. We, everyone, should have been in school.[52]

"Amen," said the NCLC. Secretary A. J. McKelway urged laws "compelling the ignorant and indifferent parent to send his children to school."[53] By 1914, only Florida, Mississippi, South Carolina, and Texas lacked compulsory education laws, although the average rural school year was still forty days shorter than the urban term. If the nation was not yet "a vast kindergarten,"[54] as Alonzo B. See of the A. B. See Elevator Company complained, at least yesterday's bonded baby slaves had been legislated into school.

To David Clark's question, "What are you going to do for them when you throw them out of the mills?"[55] the child-savers shouted with vigor, "Educate them!" (In 1918, the NCLC joined with the National Education Association to propose the creation of a federal Department of Education.) "To keep the child from going to work," wrote historian Walter Trattner, "they had to follow him into the school, the street, and the home."[56] Families might resist remodeling at first, but not to worry: in NCLC executive Gertrude Folks Zimand's chilling aphorism, "Laws make morals."[57]

That faith in the state as the fount of all things good, suffused *Children in Bondage*, a 1914 tract coauthored by poet Edwin Markham, Denver judge Benjamin Lindsey, and George Creel, later propagandist-in-chief for President Woodrow Wilson's notorious Committee on Public Information. This remarkable best-seller contains wild assertions—"the average life of the children after they go into the mills is four years"[58]; three of five home-knitters die of tuberculosis[59]—that rival Creel's later concoctions of rampaging Huns and the villainy of Eugene V. Debs.

The book reads like a purple parody: apple-cheeked munchkins peer into "the crater of death,"[60] while "greed plays with loaded dice and the little player loses all."[61] But shorn of its goofy grandiloquence, *Children in Bondage* offers us a frank, progressive view of child, parent, and state.

The authors are particularly exercised over "homework," that is, the embroidering, stitching, and making of artificial flowers and such by mothers and their tots in tenements. Homework was nigh-impossible to regulate; New York law, for instance, required only that a tenement be "sanitary." Once her building was licensed, a mother could direct her children as she pleased.

Markham tells of a widow who applied for a homework permit in New York City. She desired to sew at home and watch over her baby while her boys attended school and sold papers at dawn and dusk. The permit was denied; the relict's home reeked of "stench and filth." So she went to work in a factory, and the boys quit school to care for the infant.

A bureaucratic injustice? No, says Markham.

> In denying to mothers the right to work at home for their helpless young, and in denying to little children the right to work for needy mothers, it may seem that the law sets a cruel foot upon the neck of the broken poor. But for the larger good of humanity these denials must be: the public and the child must be protected, and the safeguard against inhumanity lies in the statute's recognition of motherhood as a service.[62]

Until the home came within the state's purview, the triune authors advised, "work on all marketed goods had to be brought into the shop and placed under factory laws."[63]

Mill apologists and hidebound states-rights Democrats were no match for the Children's Crusaders, whose progress was braked, only for a time, by the men in the White House. Disregarding the 1912 Republican platform, President Taft opposed federal child-labor legislation as unconstitutional.[64] His successor, Woodrow Wilson, agreed. (The Virginian in Wilson surfaced at the oddest times.)

Hopeful that the president had shed his strict-constructionist skin—the awesome responsibilities of office are a molting force—a delegation of social workers came a-calling, soliciting support for Congressman A. Mitchell Palmer's NCLC-drafted child-labor bill. Palmer, a Pennsylvania Democrat and future attorney general, from which position he orchestrated the Red Scare, sought to ban the interstate transport of articles produced by (1) children under fourteen who worked in factories or under sixteen who toiled in mines; (2) children under sixteen who worked more than eight hours a day; or (3) children under sixteen who worked between 7:00 P.M. and 7:00 A.M. Only about 150,000 of the land's two million young workers would be affected; the army of newsboys and farm kids and bowling-pin setters was beyond the edifying reach of Mr. Palmer's bill. (By 1912, thirty-one and twenty-two states already met the mine and factory standards, respectively; thirty-one states had adopted the eight-hour day, and twenty-eight had banned night work for minors.)

The measure was flatly unconstitutional, Wilson lectured his suppli-
cants, but he pledged neutrality.[65] The Palmer bill passed the lame-duck
House in February 1915, 233 to 43, over the protests of south Atlantic
legislators, who prevented a companion Senate bill from coming to the
floor.

The measure sailed through the next Congress, passing the House 337
to 46 and the Senate 52 to 12. The debate was brief and insipid; Congressman George F. O'Shaunessy (D-RI) confidently asserted that "this bill is
in line with the enlightened progress of the age; in line with advanced
thought."[66] His colleague C. F. Reavis (R-NE) added, "Down deep in the
subsconscious of the childhood of America lies embryonic greatness."[67]
(If nothing else, the *Congressional Record* of the era confirms the brilli-
ancy of Sinclair Lewis's ear. Like the fatuous hero of Lewis's novel, these
men knew Coolidge.)

Out of the feeble murmuring opposition one voice carried. Pitchfork
Ben Tillman, the NCLC pioneer, staked his position:

> The United States had assumed the right to enter the homes of the
> people and tell them how they must rear their children, and how,
> when, and where they must work them. . . . The Prussianizing of our
> free Republic will have begun. Little by little the Central Govern-
> ment would finally assume all the powers of Government, the
> States would sink to the level of mere counties, and Washington's
> control over the remainder of the country would be not less com-
> plete than Berlin's over all of Germany.[68]

President Wilson, locked in a tight race with progressive Republican
Charles E. Hughes, reversed field. He signed the bill, with the rather un-
seemly boast, "I congratulate the country and felicitate myself."[69]

Southern textile operative David Clark hunted up a North Carolina
mill worker, Roland Dagenhart, whose thirteen-year-old son, John,
would be fired and whose fifteen-year-old son, Reuben, would see his
daily hours cut from eleven to eight.[70] Federal Judge James E. Boyd of
the western district of North Carolina pronounced the law unconstitutional; so, too, on June 3, 1918, did the Supreme Court.

The Court's 5 to 4 decision was written by Justice William Rufus
"Good" Day, a Ravenna, Ohio, attorney whose "faith in the small town as
a symbol of the American brand of democracy"[71] yielded his distrust of all
centralized power, political and economic. Under such a broad reading of
the interstate commerce clause, Day wrote, "freedom of commerce will be
at an end, and the power of the States over local matters may be elimi-
nated, and thus our system of government be practically destroyed."[72]

Progressives were aghast. In *The New Republic*, Edwin S. Corwin
fumed, "At a moment when the government is directing the mines, the

factories, and the farms of the nation, is saying what price producers shall receive for their products, is conscripting the manhood of the country for the national armies, it is informed that it cannot regulate commerce with the end in view of conserving the health of those of whom its future armies must be composed."[73]

A new tack was chosen. Our future soldiers would be protected by Senator Atlee Pomerene (D-OH), who proposed to levy a 10 percent tax on the net profits of those industries whose practices violated the standards of the Palmer bill. The Senate approved Pomerene's amendment by 50 to 12 on December 18, 1918; friendly organs christened it "the children's Christmas present." The House voted 312 to 11 for Pomerene's tax, and President Wilson signed it into law on February 24, 1919.

Again, southern textile manufacturers found an aggrieved family to challenge the law; again, Judge Boyd voided the law in western North Carolina; again, the Supreme Court heard the case; again, the high court struck down the law, this time by a vote of 8 to 1. This time, most liberals concurred with the Court; Felix Frankfurter called Pomerene's levy "a dishonest use of the taxing power." He advised his nationalizing friends at *The New Republic*, "We must pay a price for Federalism."[74]

Discouraged reformers turned to their last resort: a constitutional amendment. The Great War had swelled the national government to an aggressive plumpness much admired by progressives. Washington had conscripted youth, set prices, and jailed dissenters. The Eighteenth Amendment had banned the sale of spirits; the Nineteenth had forced refractory states to grant women the vote; a twentieth amendment giving Congress the power to regulate child labor seemed a small step indeed. The Bourbons were weary; as one dejected state legislator whined, "They have taken our women away from us by constitutional amendment; they have taken our liquor away from us; and now they want to take our children."[75]

The centralizing trend seemed inexorable. Localism's disrepute was such that Children's Bureau chief Grace Abbott could say, "The issue of states' rights has never been raised on behalf of a good cause."[76]

The push for an amendment began as the child labor force was shrinking apace. State laws had been toughened: all but two states now banned children under fourteen from the factories, and thirty states had adopted the eight-hour day.

The number of working minors had fallen from 1.99 million (18.4% of all children) in 1910 to 1.06 million (8.5%) in 1920. Far and away the majority of this million (647,000) labored on farms—90 percent of them on their parents' land. The percentage of children aged ten to fifteen who worked at nonagricultural jobs had slipped from 7.1 in 1900 to 5.2 in 1910 and 3.3 in 1920.

Bub Mell had entered public school. Barely 20,000 youngsters were employed as cotton mill operatives in 1920; fewer than 6,000 worked in the coal mines.

The South—the godforsaken South, as it was known in Northeastern salons—was still considered the suburb of Gehenna. Alabama and South Carolina led the country in child workers (24%), but the vast majority of these were farm kids. Discounting agricultural labor, the South had proportionately fewer young toilers than the Middle Atlantic, the East North Central, or even the New England states.[77]

More than a score of amendment resolutions were introduced; the principal sponsors were Congressman Israel Foster (R-OH) and Senators Medill McCormick (R-IL) and Samuel Shortlidge (R-CA). As reported onto the House and Senate floors, the amendment read:

Section 1. The Congress shall have the power to limit, regulate, and prohibit the labor of persons under eighteen years of age.
Section 2. The power of the several states is unimpaired by this article except that the operation of State laws shall be suspended to the extent necessary to give effect to legislation enacted by the Congress.[78]

Two features gave lukewarm supporters pause. First, the use of eighteen years instead of sixteen. Secretary of Commerce Herbert Hoover, among others, counseled the tenderer age, but, he later recalled, "the lunatic fringe was demanding two years more than was attainable."[79]

Second, the use of the term "labor" rather than "employment" was a tactical—and revealing—blunder. Only now, after twenty years of agitation by the NCLC and the Hull Housers, did ordinary Americans catch a hint that the child-labor movement had grander aims than simply taking Amanda out of the mill.

Grace Abbott was responsible for the substitution: she explained, "Children often work with their parents, and are not on the payroll."[80] Mary Kilbreth of the *Woman Patriot* immediately grasped the import of the word "labor": "A girl making the bed or washing the dishes. That is labor. Or a boy helping his father milk the cows."[81] Surely these homely chores were not to be brought within Washington's bailiwick—or were they?

Congressional hearings gave the barest foretaste of the coming fight. Virtually every civic organization in the land lined up behind the child labor amendment: the National Education Association, the American Legion, the Camp Fire Girls, the League of Women Voters, the Women's Christian Temperance Union, the PTA, the YWCA—even Presidents Warren Harding and Calvin Coolidge.

The two best-known witnesses against the amendment, *Southern Textile Bulletin* editor David Clark and James A. Emery of the National Association of Manufacturers, were dismissed as mouthpieces of the child-exploiters. Also testifying were a stream of obscure self-styled "constitutionalists," most of them from Sopping Wet Maryland.[82] They were paid little heed, but they adumbrated two of the most devastating anti-amendment themes.

First—and no one disputed this—is that the child labor amendment was cousin-german to Prohibition. Drunkard fathers necessitated the Eighteenth Amendment; indolent dads would force the twentieth upon us.[83] American men were dissolute bums whose failings cried out for Washington's remedies. (All the amendments in the world, though, can't crush the resilient family. My maternal grandmother, Mary Stella Baker, spent her girlhood picking dandelions that were transubstantiated into wine in her parents' speakeasy. Take *that*, eighteenth and twentieth manque amendments.)

The second discordant note was introduced by Willis R. Jones, representing the Women's Constitutional League of Maryland: "The fathers and the mothers are better prepared to pass judgement upon the needs and the welfare of their children than this Congress is, or than the Children's Bureau. I know not who the Children's Bureau is composed of: I have heard intimations that there are not many mothers connected with [it]."[84]

The charge that proamendment women were hyprocrite humanitarians who bled for the abstraction "child" but blanched at real, live, fleshy, bloody tykes was rude—and clever—and partly true. When American Bar Association president Clarence E. Martin referred to "the maiden ladies resident in Hull House, Chicago . . . a hotbed of radicalism,"[85] the implication was clear: the child-savers were officious spinsters, lesbians, and Reds.

Grace Abbott, Lillian Wald, Jane Addams, Julia Lathrop, Katharine Lumpkin, Florence Kelley: Messrs. Martin and Jones, however tactless, had a point. National Consumers League chief Kelley, the amendment's lobbyist-dynamo, had been a fervid Socialist Laborite until she was expelled by the party on the (possibly trumped-up) charge of misusing funds.

Marcet Haldeman-Julius, Jane Addams's niece, told of visiting her "Aunt Jenny" at Hull House and finding her distant, impersonal, cold.

> "She isn't a very auntly person," I (aged six) complained to my mother on one of our visits.
> "That," I was informed in a tone of rebuke, "is because she is aunt to so many. She hasn't much time for each of you."[86]

The childlessness of the child-savers became a favorite refrain. Pennsylvanian Edward J. Maginnis wrote in a widely circulated open letter:

"One class of citizens composed principally of cultured men and women of small or no families at all, living in comfort, albeit with good intentions, are attempting to force legislation on the industrial class, composed mostly of humble, stalwart men and women of large families."[87]

The *Woman Patriot*, an anti-suffrage organ refitted for the broader "defense of the family against the state," entered the fray with articles alternately cogent and screed-like. Miss Mary C. Kilbreth, its president, picked up the ball carried years before by Senator Weldon Heyburn. "As women," she testified, "we are particularly concerned [about] the right of castle aspect of this amendment."[88]

This phrase, worn threadbare over the next year, drove reformers up the wall. "The home is the castle!" jeered two socialist researchers. "Have they seen the 'castles' out of which child workers come?"[89] Shiftless or absent fathers; overworked skeletal mothers; poor little Bub Mell in his fetid cell, his mill town hell, a slangy kid headed for the pen.

Labor for teenagers did find its defenders. "Give the children a chance to work," pleaded the principal of a girls' trade school. "Give at least as much attention to fostering work habits in all as we give to restrictive legislation which affects relatively few."[90]

Miss Kilbreth of the *Woman Patriot* declared:

We are oppressed with white collarism. It is absurd that we Americans, who are supposed to be a democracy, have a contempt for manual work. . . . We have been a resourceful, self-reliant, energetic people, and I contend that this amendment would result in the practical-minded children becoming idlers and loafers, and by the implied stigma on work in this amendment there would be more overcerebralized young intellectuals, from whom the radicals are recruited and who are the curse of society.[91]

Miss Kilbreth and others unbeholden to industrial interests saw child labor as good and proper to a Jeffersonian America. Elders taught skills to youngsters that would enable them to live, in adulthood, as independent freeholders, sturdy hard-working unbought and unbossed citizens of the republic. The Hamiltonian uses of children—as cogs in a mighty industrial empire—went undefended in the 1920s. David Clark and the National Association of Manufacturers played states-rights tunes instead.

Kilbrethians saluted the salutary effects of wholesome work. Senator Bayard reminded scripture-spouting legislators that "as a boy of 12 Jesus worked in a carpenter's shop. . . . He received no detriment from doing so, and He grew up to be the most wonderful man in the world."[92] No one dared gainsay Bayard.

But carpenters and mill hands were small in number; the vast majority of "child workers" were farm boys and girls. Grace Abbott assured solons that banning field work was the furthest thing from her mind, but the amendment mustn't exempt agriculture because, well, who knew what conditions would obtain in rural America in fifty years? (That rural America would very nearly cease to exist occurred to no one.)

Miss Abbott may have been an honest sort—although immediately after the amendment's death she announced her support for federal regulation of family farm labor. Her comrades, though, were either disingenuous or liars. NCLC Secretary Lovejoy, for instance, claimed that "the farm child is frequently getting too much work, too little schooling, and too little developmental care. . . . He is too often a mere drudge who will grow up an ignorant, inefficient worker."[93] Yet Lovejoy hastened to add: "There is no thought on the part of advocates of this amendment to have the Federal Government interfere with the conditions of children on farms."[94]

The NCLC disgorged study after study confirming the dreariness of the georgic world and the imbecility of its inmates. E. C. Lindeman found that "farm life in general does not produce a degree of mental alertness and neuro-muscular co-ordination essential to an enthusiastic and optimistic outlook on life."[95]

The romantic vision of an American arcadia was a joke; its cultured defenders were "typewriter agrarians," scoffed H. L. Mencken. Twenty years earlier Populist Tom Watson had complained, "It takes these city fellows to draw ideal pictures of farm life—pictures which are no more true to real life than a Fashion Plate is to an actual man or woman."[96] Not to worry, Tom: the slickers soon realized that the valley of democracy was filled with morons. Progress kicked small farmers into towns that more often resembled Winesburg than Friendship Village. However unwittingly—Edgar Lee Masters, after all, was a Jeffersonian, and Mencken an anarchist—the debunkers of rural virtue blazed a path for the Remolders.

With deliberate speed, the Grange and the American Farm Bureau Federation rolled into opposition. Amendment foes had found their hook: defense of the forty-acre farm family. Congressman Fritz G. Lanham (D-TX) brought down the House with his mock psalm:

Consider the Federal agent in the field; he toils not, nor does he spin; and yet I say unto you that even Solomon in all his populous household was not arrayed with powers like one of these.

Children, obey your agents from Washington, for this is right.

Honor thy father and thy mother, for the Government has created them but a little lower than the Federal agent. Love, honor, and disobey them.

Whatsoever thy hand findeth to do, tell it to thy father and mother and let them do it.

Six days shalt thou do all thy rest, and on the seventh day thy parents shall rest with thee.

Go to the bureau officer, thou sluggard; consider his ways and be idle.

Toil, thou farmer's wife; thou shalt have no servant in thy house, nor let thy children help thee.

And all thy children shall be taught of the Federal agent, and great shall be the peace of thy children.

Thy children shall rise up and call the Federal agent blessed.[97]

How odd, how unsettling for us, in this age of the DEA (Drug Enforcement Administration) and the IRS, to read of the deep-seated antipathy that conservatives of the 1920s had for federal officers. Some warned of "house-to-house and farm-to-farm searches for youthful workers."[98] The *Woman Patriot* previsioned "vicious espionage and invasion of the homes of the people in violation of Article IV of the Bill of Rights by swarms of bureaucrats from Washington with inquisitorial powers. It is absurd to pretend that these salaried professional humanitarians would have the interest of the youth of distant States as much at heart as the mothers who bore them or the communities in which they live."[99]

(The cost of administering these laws, through a host of bureaus and agents, never became an issue. When nagged for a dollar estimate, Grace Abbott sighed, "I would hate to have any cost value put on what we were doing for the child."[100] Plus ça change.)

Burlesques and dire prophecies were—as yet—no match for the child-savers. The House approved the Child Labor Amendment on April 26, 1924, by a vote of 297 to 69.[101]

The outstanding Senate foe of the amendment was James Wadsworth (R-NY), issue of the Genesee Valley's hoariest aristocrats. Although detested by many of their neighbors as fox-hunting twits who abused the hired help in phony accents, the Wadsworths, like many old families, had an admirable sense of civic-mindedness, an almost proprietary feeling toward the republic.

The old America was slipping away from Wadsworth; his revered Constitution had become the instrument of wrenching social change. "We are whittling away at the structure established by the fathers," the Senator lamented. "If we whittle long enough, we will destroy it."[102]

Wadsworth had special loathing for uplifters and their constitutional amendments. He was New York's most vocal Wet; he and his wife, the daughter of John Hay, were the country's leading anti–woman suffrage couple. Now came yet another amendment striking at local rule—which in the Genesee Valley meant Wadsworth rule.[103]

Although his motley Senate coalition was defeated on June 2, 1924, by a vote of 61 to 23, James Wadsworth introduced an issue that would, in six months time, scuttle the Child Labor Amendment. Congress, he predicted, would someday legislate "that no person of 17 years of age . . . shall be permitted to do a certain kind of work unless that person had a certain kind of education; not only a certain amount of schooling but the *kind* of schooling."[104]

American Catholicism waked. The Church was besieged on several fronts. Prohibition was widely regarded as a swipe against "rum and romanism." The Klan was enjoying a brief resurgence. New York governor Al Smith had been denied the 1924 Democratic nomination for president partly on the papist question.

Even more alarming, Oregon had effectively outlawed private schools in a 1922 initiative. (The Oregon law, which required children between the ages of eight and sixteen to attend public schools, was struck down in 1925 by a unanimous Supreme Court in *Pierce v. Society of Sisters.*) A similar initiative was on the Michigan ballot in November 1924; anti-Catholics and Progressives had declared war on the parochial school.[105]

By the time the child labor amendment was sent to the forty-eight states, a massive shift in popular sentiment was underway. The opposition had once consisted of mill owners and southern politicians whose valentines to the Anti-Saloon League made their orotund invocations of states rights seem like so much fustian. Now, as the amendment came before state legislatures, a fresh coalition assembled: the Catholic Church, farmers, antifeminists, northern Mugwumps (Senator Wadsworth, Nicholas Murray Butler, Elihu Root), and ordinary families afeard of the encroachment of the state and childless do-gooders. Bub Mell's dad was fighting back.

Arkansas was the first state to ratify the amendment, in late June, after which, the deluge. State after state, including progressive bastions, rejected the measure. In Georgia, where the repudiation was unanimous, State Representative McCorsey declared: "I don't want any more monkeying with the buzz-saw by that bunch in Washington. We don't mix nohow. We weren't born under the same regime and don't drink out of the same bottle."[106] The suspicion that Massachusetts manufacturers were pulling the strings remained strong in the Confederacy. South Carolina's Senator Dial excoriated "the mill people of New England, who are jealous of the prosperity and progress the South has made."[107] Well, maybe. A Tyro, Ohio, state legislator named Robert Taft, for instance, supported the amendment "on the practical grounds that it would help Cincinnati industries meet unfair competition from other states."[108]

Backers were taken aback. They had predicted swift ratification; the journal *Survey* had foreseen only "the familiar bogeys . . . of states' rights, the prohibition analogy, the grasping bureaucrats of Washington, [and] the sacred right of the 17-year-old farmer-boy to pick blueberries on the hill."[109]

How reasonable were the fears of amendment foes? How justified were their alarums? Certainly the farmers had cause to worry. Children helping their parents in fields and barns must be rescued and spirited into schools, reformers insisted, and if the local economy depended on their labor at harvest time, then perhaps the local economy ought to be modernized. A New Jersey cranberry bog owner's protests fell on deaf ears: "If man-made laws about when children must attend school are in conflict with God-made laws about when the crops shall ripen, then the laws of God must be obeyed."[110]

The other, more speculative backroads fear, as expressed by the editors of *Power Farming*, was that the amendment would grant Congress "the power to forbid any farm boy from milking a cow or even driving in a cow from the pasture until he is eighteen years old. . . . It might and probably would be made illegal for sister Susie to wash a dish or sew on a button until after her eighteenth birthday."[111]

This was an exaggeration; even Edwin Markham saw nothing wrong with washing the dishes. (Hoeing was another matter.) But *Power Farming* was right: the amendment *did* grant that power—to a Congress that had so recently torn boys from their homes and communities and sent them across a vast ocean to die, or to return to a country in which bottles of beer were contraband. As New York attorney Austen F. Fox drily commented, "Granting power is not the best way to prevent its exercise."[112]

And what of the claims made by the *Woman Patriot* that governmental authority would supersede parental authority? That, as Senator James A. Reed (D-MO) feared, Congress would "trample upon the institution of the home; and establish an offensive and tyrannical socialism on the soil that was redeemed to freedom and that has been consecrated to individual liberty."[113]

Even moderate Raymond G. Fuller, NCLC research director, admitted

If it is unsafe to leave children to the mercies of business for profit, so it is to leave their protection even to so great and beneficient a force in the life of mankind as parental love. . . . We must limit parental freedom as well as employers' freedom, but the main thing is to aid and strengthen the home—for the children's sake. The virtue of laws . . . is to make legal prohibitions and compulsions less and less necessary, through having promoted the intelligence of the makers of homes.[114]

(Or "laws make morals," in Ms. Zimand's pungent adage.)

Amendment advocates were determined to nurture some embryonic greatness, and if a few doors had to be kicked in, well, that's advanced thinking for you. A popular theory (they didn't have "paradigms" then)

was "Government as Overparent." Denver judge Ben Lindsey, coauthor of *Children in Bondage*, believed that "an economic earthquake has shaken the 'old home' to pieces. The foundations are crumbled, the walls are spread, the winds of the world blow through. . . . The Nation, the State, the municipality, these have stepped in, assumed practical control of the family in its most intimate relations, and are overparents."[115]

Just how far this overparenting might go was unclear. Florence Kelley, Socialist Laborite bête-noire to the *Woman Patriot*, envisioned virtually no limits on the powers of the central authority. Suffragette Alice Paul, a marginal figure in this debate, insisted that "the State assume *entire* responsibility for the maintenance and education of children"[116] (my italics).

Charlotte Perkins Gilman had depicted the family of the future in *The Home: Its Work and Influence*. Decrying "the archaic cult of home-worship,"[117] Gilman urged housewives to turn over their two most time-consuming domestic duties (child rearing and cooking) to trained experts, versed in the advanced scientific thought of the age. Dinner would be eaten in large communal eateries; infants would be cared for by professionals in nurseries. For too long American women had given us dyspepsia and spoiled brats; indeed, "that the care and education of children have developed at all is due to the intelligent efforts of doctors, nurses, [and] teachers."[118]

Home, in Gilman's view, stifled "social consciousness." We become excessively attached to other members of the family, and disregard the outer world. "Christ rose above all family ties,"[119] she pointed out; oughtn't we be Christ-like?

Once freed from the confinement of home, from the tedium of cooking and mothering, American women would take their rightful place in industrial society. Children, no longer dependent upon ignorant mamas lacking college degrees, would emerge "from the very lowest grade of private ownership into the safe, broad level of common citizenship. That which no million separate families could give their millions of separate children, the state can give."[120]

In Gilman's view—largely shared by the Hull Housers who ran the Children's Bureau—the federal government had not only the right but the obligation to intervene in family relations. And yes, if science determined that sewing buttons was bad for Susie, then Susie's mom must be prevented from passing on seamstress work to the poor girl.

In the aftermath of war, in the midst of Prohibition, on the cusp of a movement (which soon fizzled) to enact national laws regulating marriage and divorce, Middle Americans were right to suspect the child labor amendment as a potentially monstrous measure. (I don't want to exaggerate the tyrannical cast of the movement, but the Torquemada and Goebbels of the late teens were A. Mitchell Palmer and George Creel, leading child-savers of the early teens. The cause did not attract men and women in whose hearts burned the love of liberty.)

The child labor amendment met its Waterloo in Massachusetts, once thought to be its stronghold. An advisory referendum was scheduled for November 4, 1924. The tea leaves betokened success: Massachusetts had been the first state to pass a strict child-labor law; Bay State mill owners were at a competitive disadvantage with southern employers; Senators Walsh and Lodge—in fact, every candidate for a major office—endorsed it.

However, a Paddy-Brahmin united front arrayed against the amendment. The Citizens' Committee to Protect Our Homes and Children, Harvard president A. Lawrence Lowell at the helm, warned of Congress interfering "in the discipline of every household. [It will] . . . take from parents the right and duty to educate and guide their children."[121]

Cardinal William O'Connell and the Archdiocese of Boston mounted a vigorous (and, outside Massachusetts, widely denounced) campaign against the amendment. On three successive Sundays, priests inveighed against the amendment from the pulpit. It would unleash "swarms of paid Governmental workers through the country," one padre contended, "seeing that parents are complying with the bureau's ideas of bringing up their children, supervising their education . . . and interfering in the sacred rights of parents."[122]

The Lutherans, if less powerful, were equally comminatory. The Lutheran Pastors of Boston declared, "We hold that the child belongs to the parents, not to the State. Any infringement of the fundamental rights of parents would be not only un-American, but also anti-Christian. . . . Bureaucrats . . . may abuse the power thus given them to destroy the Family and the Church."[123]

(Lutherans were decisive in defeating the measure in Nebraska and Missouri. While Oregon was trying to shut down Catholic schools, Nebraska was prohibiting the teaching of any foreign language—read: German—to elementary students and teaching in any foreign language to students of all ages. The Nebraska law was struck down by the Supreme Court in *Meyer v. State of Nebraska*, 1923.)

The child labor amendment died in Massachusetts, 697,563 to 241,461.[124] It was done in by Catholics and Mugwumps and farmers. That canniest of pols, Boston mayor James Curley, apostasized and presided over the amendment's last hurrah. The rebuke—the jaw-dropping magnitude of the defeat—staggered observers. (See the 1975 New York referendum on a state equal rights amendment for an uncanny parallel.)

The Massachusetts shot was heard 'round the country. New York governor Al Smith, whilom champion of the amendment, backpedaled. When he proposed an advisory referendum for New York, Florence Kelley threw a termagant fit. Convinced that working-class Catholics and the mossback cretinage of Upstate would sink the measure, Miss Kelley set out to collect the signatures of 100,000 "leading citizens"— beginning with Mrs. John D. Rockefeller, Jr. Her tony petition drive fizzled; no referendum was held; New York never ratified.[125] (Indeed, when the amendment recrudesced in the mid-1930s, Al Smith was among its fieriest foes.)

Miss Kelley's undemocratic folly was no aberration. Frustrated by the amendment's failure to excite enthusiasm outside of Hull House, reformers itched for an iron heel. Fumed Henry F. Pringle: "The fact of the matter is that I haven't much faith in the States. I don't think they are entitled to their 'rights' when they fail to exercise them."[126] Or as Raymond G. Fuller put it, "there is no democracy in permitting backward localities to use up childhood."[127]

By Christmas 1925, just four states—Arkansas, Arizona, California, and Wisconsin—had ratified the would-be twentieth amendment. Montana and Colorado later made it a sextet, but twenty years of prologue had led to—rout. The amendment was killed, establishment historiography has it, by "reactionary religious elements and the rural and business interests."[128]

The amendment jerked back to life in 1933. Swayed by the labor-union argument that children were stealing scarce jobs from adults, fourteen states ratified the amendment in the New Deal's first year. (By 1933, every state had enacted a compulsory school attendance law covering youths up to the age of fourteen, so legislation was less necessary than ever before.)

On a parallel track, the rule of ukase was picking up steam. Under the National Recovery Act (NRA), the Roosevelt administration imposed a nationwide "code of competition" that forbade children under sixteen from working in any mining or manufacturing industry, and limited those between the ages of fourteen and sixteen to three-hour workdays between the morning and vespertinal seven o'clocks. More than 150,000 youngsters were thrown out of work, prompting NCLC general secretary Courtenay Dinwiddie to rhapsodize, "We have done more to eliminate child labor in the last three or four months than we were able to do in the preceding ten years."[129] Ah, the joys of executive fiat!

Although President Franklin Roosevelt announced, "Child labor is abolished,"[130] in his 1934 State of the Union address, the amendment trudged on. Four more states ratified over the next two years.

Anti-amendment forces regrouped, led by an eminence grise quartet: Harvard President Lowell, Columbia University President Butler, American Bar Association President Martin, and statesman Elihu Root, whose place in the Senate James Wadsworth had taken.[131]

Martin, in a nationwide radio address, argued that under the amendment, "the children of the nation can be Russianized. . . . Military training can be made compulsory. . . . Congress shall acquire over children the primary power parents now have."[132] (As the teens had given way to the 1920s and 1930s, "Russianized" had replaced "Prussianized" as the totalitarian verb of choice.)

Amusingly, the newspapers, after ten years of flacking for the amendment, did a collective flip-flop. An NRA newspaper code had been adopted in February 1934: to combat the scourge of juvenile delinquency, paper boys in cities of 50,000 had to be at least fourteen; in smaller burgs, these Ragged Dicks had to be twelve. Newsgirls were subjected to even stricter standards.

Upon the promulgation of the NRA newsboy code, sixty papers that had championed the amendment as late as 1933 now gravely editorialized against it as being subversive of all that is good and American.[133] (The most shameless volte-face was done by the *Chicago Tribune*, whose co-owner Medill McCormick had sponsored the amendment in the Senate.)

The NRA was struck down by the Supreme Court in 1935, spurring four more states to ratify the amendment, upping the total to 28. And there the drive stalled.

Restrictions similar to those in the old Palmer bill were incorporated into the Fair Labor Standards Act of 1938. When the FSLA was upheld by a chastened Court, *Hammer v. Dagenhart* was laid to rest at last.

The FSLA did exempt children employed by their parents: the NCLC criticized this "loophole"[134] and Grace Abbott, erstwhile professor of the sanctity of the family farm, fretted that "agricultural work is not adequately controlled."[135] But the original goals of the child-savers had been achieved. The amendment—eight states shy of enshrinement in the Constitution—was interred. "Finally," announced NCLC chairman Homer Folks, "in 1938, the long battle was won."[136]

Historian Richard B. Sherman has noted, "The fight for the amendment scattered rather than consolidated . . . the old progressive coalition."[137] Nationalizers and centralizers split with antimonopolists such as Senator Borah, who called the amendment "the most pronounced invasion of local self-government that has ever been proposed."[138] The rift foreshadowed the breakup of the progressive coalition in the late 1930s over the New Deal and U.S. involvement in the Second World War. With the Child Labor Amendment, the battle between partisans of the old republic and the new republic was joined.

Industrial child labor was ended, but the sacred right of the seventeen-year-old boy to pick blueberries, at least on his own farm, remained intact. Those who would overrun the poor man's castle would acquire many new weapons, but a child labor amendment battering ram was not among them.

Opposition to the amendment had united, in common—and success-ful—cause, an extraordinary coalition: rural southern Protestants, northern working-class Catholics, antifeminists, localist Progressives, domestic manufacturers, farmers, and Mugwump wisemen. Together, they defeated a measure that had virtually the entire political establish-ment behind it.

A pity that the coalition has never re-formed.

NOTES

1. Quoted in Clarke A. Chambers, *Seedtime of Reform* (Minneapo-lis: University of Minnesota Press, 1963), pp. 45–46.

2. Claudius O. Johnson, *Borah of Idaho* (New York: Longmans, Green & Co., 1936), p. 188.

3. Quoted in Walter I. Trattner, *Crusade for the Children* (Chi-cago: Quadrangle, 1970), p. 199.

4. *Congressional Record*, May 31, 1924, p. 10001.

5. Edwin Markham, Benjamin B. Lindsey, and George Creel, *Children in Bondage* (New York: Hearst's International Library, 1914), p. 41.

6. Quoted in Richard B. Sherman, "The Rejection of the Child La-bor Amendment," *Mid-America*, January 1963, pp. 9–10.

7. Quoted in Grace Abbott, *The Child and the State*, vol. 1 (Chi-cago: University of Chicago Press, 1938), p. 277.

8. Quoted in John Spargo, *The Bitter Cry of the Children* (New York: Macmillan, 1906), p. 128.

9. Horatio Alger, *Ragged Dick* (New York: Macmillan, 1962/ 1867), p. 46. Alger, a benefactor of the Children's Aid Society, was no lackey of the Exploiters. He successfully lobbied the New York State legislature to criminalize the "padrone" system by which unscrupulous adults pimped out immigrant children. Horatio, alas, took too great a shine to boys: his pederasty got him booted out of his Unitarian minis-try in Brewster, Massachusetts, which is why he took up writing as a career. Edwin P. Hoyt, *Horatio's Boys* (Radnor, Pa.: Chilton Book Co., 1974), pp. 4–6.

10. Elizabeth Stuart Phelps, *The Silent Partner* (Boston: James R. Osgood & Co., 1871), p. 48.

11. Vernon Parrington, *Main Currents in American Thought*, vol. 3 (New York: Harcourt, Brace & Co., 1927), p. 61.

12. *Bartlett's Familiar Quotations*, 15th ed. (Boston: Little, Brown, 1980), p. 351.

13. Phelps, pp. 107–8.

14. Quoted in Katharine DuPre Lumpkin and Dorothy Wolff Douglas, *Child Workers in America* (New York: Robert M. McBride Co., 1937), p. 222.

15. Quoted in Raymond G. Fuller, *Child Labor and the Constitution* (New York: Thomas Y. Crowell Co., 1923), pp. 37–38.

16. Hamlin Garland, *A Son of the Middle Border* (New York: P. F. Collier & Son, 1917), pp. 100–101.

17. Quoted in Fuller, p. 35.

18. Trattner, p. 40.

19. Quoted in Stephen B. Wood, *Constitutional Politics in the Progressive Era* (Chicago: University of Chicago Press, 1968), p. 257.

20. *Congressional Record*, January 28, 1907, p. 1801.

21. Quoted in *Child Labor and Social Progress* (New York: National Child Labor Committee, 1908), p. 8. Senator Beveridge, the Teddy Roosevelt Progressive whose pet causes were child labor and imperialism, wailed, "whereas the children of the white working people of the South are going to the mill and to decay, the Negro children are going to school and improvement." Quoted in Markham et al., p. 332.

22. Edgar Gardner Murphy, *The Present South* (New York: Macmillan, 1904), p. 140.

23. *Child Labor and Social Progress*, p. 70.

24. Murphy, p. 108.

25. *Congressional Record*, February 2, 1916, p. 2013.

26. John Steinbeck, *The Grapes of Wrath* (New York: Viking, 1958 [1939]), p. 306.

27. Dorothy Dunbar Bromley, "The Newspapers and Child Labor," *The Nation*, January 30, 1935, p. 131.

28. Markham et al., p. 226.

29. Spargo, p. 185.

30. Josephine Goldmark, "Street Labor and Juvenile Delinquency," *Political Science Quarterly*, September 1904, p. 424.

31. *Congressional Record*, January 28, 1907, p. 1800.

32. Albert Beveridge, introduction to *The Cry of the Children*, by Mrs. John Van Vorst (New York: Moffat, Yard & Co., 1908), p. xv.

33. *Congressional Record*, January 28, 1907, pp. 1800–1801.

34. Murphy wrote, "The conditions of industry vary so greatly and so decisively from State to State and from locality to locality" that uniform laws were in no wise desirable. Murphy, p. 129.

35. The American Federation of Labor opposed Beveridge. President Samuel Gompers feared "it would set a dangerous precedent and that further government interference in labor relations might follow." The union shortly thereafter reversed itself in the hope that barring child labor would drive up adult wages. Trattner, p. 89.

36. *Congressional Record*, January 8, 1912, p. 704.

37. Ibid.

38. *Congressional Record*, January 30, 1912, pp. 1526–27.

39. *Congressional Record*, January 8, 1912, pp. 704–5.

40. *Congressional Record*, January 31, 1912, pp. 1576–78.

41. Thomas Robinson Dawley, Jr., *The Child that Toileth Not* (New York: Gracia Publishing Co., 1912), p. 7.

42. Ibid., p. 64.

43. Ibid., p. 30.

44. Ibid., p. 227.

45. Ibid., p. 243.

46. See William P. Few, "The Constructive Philanthropy of a Southern Cotton Mill," *South Atlantic Quarterly*, January 1909, pp. 82–90.

47. Quoted in Abbott, pp. 477–78.

48. Julia Magruder, "The Child Labor Problem: Fact Versus Sentimentality," *North American Review*, October 1907, p. 245.

49. Ibid., pp. 248–51.

50. Trattner, p. 40.

51. Markham et al., p. 373.

52. Quoted in Victoria Byerly, *Hard Times Cotton Mill Girls* (Ithaca, N.Y.: ILR Press, 1986), p. 65.

53. Quoted in *Child Labor and Social Progress*, p. 27.

54. Quoted in Chambers, p. 38.

55. Quoted in Lumpkin and Douglas, p. 225.

56. Trattner, p. 154.

57. Quoted in Chambers, p. 47.

58. Markham et al., p. 47.

59. Ibid., p. 87.

60. Ibid., p. 58.

61. Ibid., p. 66.

62. Ibid., pp. 180–81. God only knows how many children helped with homework. The U.S. Census Bureau didn't. In 1909, New York City's diligent inspectors issued 11,162 tenement licenses. Mary Van Kleeck, "Child Labor in Home Industries," *Annals of the American Academy of Political and Social Science*, March 1910, pp. 145–49.

63. Trattner, p. 148. Some early opponents of homework argued from a profamily position, which their modern heirs have abandoned. For a provocative interpretation of the homework debate, then and now, see Allan C. Carlson, *Family Questions* (New Brunswick, N.J.: Transaction, 1988), pp. 139–54.

64. Taft was the last president wholeheartedly to oppose federal legislation. In prose as sluggish as his gait, he wrote,

It seeks indirectly and by duress, to compel the States to pass a certain kind of legislation that is completely within their discretion to enact or not. Child labor in the State of the shipment has no legitimate or germane relation to the interstate commerce of which the goods thus made are to form a part, to its character or to its effect. Such an attempt of Congress to use its power of regulating such commerce to suppress the use of child labor in the State of shipment would be a clear usurpation of that State's rights.

William Howard Taft, *Popular Government* (New Haven, Conn.: Yale University Press, 1913), pp. 142–43.

In his 1908 treatise *Constitutional Government*, Wilson wrote,

The proposed federal . . . regulation of child labor affords a striking example. If the power to regulate commerce between the states can be stretched to include the regulation of labor in mills and factories, it can be made to embrace every particular of the industrial organization and action of the country. The only limitations Congress would observe, should the Supreme Court assent to such obviously absurd extravagancies of interpretation, would be the limitations of opinion and circumstance.

Woodrow Wilson, *Constitutional Government* (New York: Columbia University Press), p. 179.

65. Arthur S. Link, *Wilson: The New Freedom* (Princeton, N.J.: Princeton University Press, 1956), p. 257.

66. *Congressional Record*, February 2, 1916, p. 2008.

67. Ibid., p. 2010.

68. *Congressional Record*, August 8, 1916, p. 12294.

69. Quoted in Trattner, p. 131.

70. Lowell Mellett of Scripps-Howard tracked down Reuben Dagenhart in 1923, on the eve of the amendment debate. Twenty years old, downcast, and living in Charlotte, Reuben felt no gratitude toward the court or his lawyers.

I don't see that I got any benefit. I guess I'd been a lot better off if they hadn't won it. Look at me! A hundred and five pounds, a grown man and no education. I may be mistaken, but I think the years I've put in in the cotton mills have stunted my growth. They kept me from getting any schooling. (Quoted in Abbott, p. 516)

71. Joseph E. McLean, *William Rufus Day: Supreme Court Judge from Ohio* (Baltimore: Johns Hopkins, 1946), p. 17.

72. Quoted in Trattner, p. 136. Day was that rarest D.C. specimen: a man of place in a high place. A village lawyer content in Ravenna and, later, Canton, Ohio, he was summoned to Washington in 1897 by his old friend William McKinley. He served with distinction as the in-house dove (McKinley's front-porch conscience?) during the Spanish-American War. President Theodore Roosevelt appointed "Good" Day to

the Supreme Court in 1902. On the bench, Day viewed "with distrust extreme concentrations of political or economic power"; though a strict constructionist of national powers, he allowed the states wide berths in the disciplining of monopolists and malefactors. Good Day was Ravenna to the core, and to the end.

73. Quoted in Wood, p. 188.

74. Ibid., p. 291.

75. Quoted in Trattner, p. 171.

76. Abbott, p. 464. Miss Abbott had an annoying—perhaps revealing—habit of using the locution "inalienable right" in a belittling way. Selfishness, ignorance, the exploitation of children: to Grace Abbott, inalienable rights were exercised, inevitably, in the service of wrong. See especially *The Child and the State*.

Even the cautious NCLC jettisoned its incrementalist, southern-sensitive strategy, causing new chairman David Franklin Houston, a Texan who was President Wilson's Secretary of Agriculture, to jump ship in 1923.

77. Fuller, pp. 7–8. The 1920 U.S. Census discovered 1.06 million children between the ages of ten and fifteen who were "gainfully employed" or who "contributed materially" to the family income. (The total population for that age group was 12.5 million.) Of this million-plus, 714,000 were boys and 346,000 were girls. More than 60 percent—647,000—were engaged in agriculture. The rest worked as or in:

Occupations	Total Number	% of Total Employed
Messenger and office boys/girls	48,028	11.6
Servants/waiters	41,586	10.1
Sales	30,370	7.3
Clerks	22,521	5.4
Cotton-mill operatives	21,875	5.3
Newsboys	20,706	5.0
Iron-steel industry operatives	12,904	3.1
Clothing industry operatives	11,757	2.8
Lumber-furniture industry operatives	10,585	2.6
Silk-mill operatives	10,023	2.4
Shoe factory operatives	7,545	1.8
Woolen-worsted machine operatives	7,077	1.7
Coal mine operatives	5,850	1.4
All other occupations	162,722	39.3

78. Resolution sponsor Israel Foster offered an expansive definition of child labor: "the work of children under conditions that interfere with the physical development, education, and opportunity for recreation which children require." How can the arduous labor on a small farm not "interfere" with "the opportunity for recreation"? *Congressional Record*, April 25, 1924, p.7177.

79. Herbert Hoover, *The Memoirs of Herbert Hoover* (New York: Macmillan, 1951), p. 102.

80. House Document 497, 68th Congress, 2d Session, *Judiciary Committee Hearings on the Proposed Child Labor Amendment to the Constitution of the United States*, p. 160.

81. Ibid., p. 161.

82. The Maryland witnesses, citizens of a state in which Governor Alfred Ritchie and H. L. Mencken were very much in the bibulous mainstream, were soberly lectured by Representative Earl Michener (R-MI) of the Judiciary Committee: "Maryland . . . made the same protest against that constitutional amendment [the Eighteenth] because it was doing something for Maryland that Maryland did not want done." House Document 497, p. 134. One poor fellow, having watched every previous amendment foe be rebuked as "wet," began his testimony, "I have never drunk a drop of beer, whisky, or wine in my life." House Document 497, p. 110.

83. To a lesser extent, ignorant immigrant men, Catholics and Jews and Italians and bohunks, were used as an argument for the Nineteenth Amendment. See Murray N. Rothbard, "The Progressive Era and the Family," in *The American Family and the State*, ed. Joseph R. Peden and Fred R. Glahe (San Francisco: Pacific Research Institute, 1986), especially pp. 122–27.

84. House Document 497, p. 104.

85. Clarence E. Martin, "Shall Americanism Remain?" *Commonweal*, April 13, 1934, p. 649.

86. Marcet Haldeman-Julius, *Jane Addams as I Knew Her* (Girard, Kans.: Julius Publications, 1936), p. 3.

87. *Congressional Record*, February 2, 1916, p. 2025.

88. House Document 497, p. 159.

89. Lumpkin and Douglas, p. 237. The prize for most curious phrasing goes to the American Federation of Teachers, which declared the amendment's purpose as "to secure to each child that opportunity to develop into a self-supporting economic unit which the American Constitution intends him to have." House Document 497, p. 260.

90. Quoted in Elizabeth Frazer, "Children and Work," *Saturday Evening Post*, April 4, 1925, p. 147.

91. House Document 497, pp. 159–60.

92. *Congressional Record*, May 31, 1924, p. 9995.

93. Owen P. Lovejoy, "Helping the Farmer through His Children," *Annals of the American Academy of Political and Social Science*, November 1921, p. 149.

94. *Congressional Record*, April 25, 1924, p. 7178.

95. Quoted in Fuller, p. 41. Not all amendment supporters dissembled. When House Judiciary committeeman W. D. Boies (R-IA) asked William P. Connery (D-MA), an amendment sponsor, "Do you not think that this regulation ought to be confined to certain sorts of work, rather than to make it so general that the boy out on the farm can refuse to get an armful of wood or a basket of eggs for his mother?" Connery replied, "I think that should be applied to the boy on the farm also." House Document 497, p. 14.

96. Quoted in C. Vann Woodward, *Tom Watson: Agrarian Rebel* (New York: Macmillan, 1938), p. 127.

97. *Congressional Record*, April 25, 1924, p. 7199. Lanham was one of the chamber's finer wits. He imagined a day when "above the fireplace, where used to hang the old familiar motto, 'What is home without a mother?' is another in its stead, which reads, 'What is home without a Federal agent?' And over the door [hangs] . . . another prayerful one, 'Bureau officer, bless our home.' " Ibid., p. 7198.

98. *Congressional Record*, May 31, 1924, p. 9976.

99. Ibid., p. 9963.

100. House Document 497, p. 53.

101. There were still localists around; their case was nicely put by Missouri congressman Harry B. Hawes: "We do not want men and women from outside of Missouri, who do not live there, who have no interests there, no local reputation, to be sent to our state to direct or regulate matters that are of purely local concern." *Congressional Record*, April 25, 1924, p. 7197.

Cant dominated the debate, though wit made an occasional cameo. When Minnesota Representative Oscar J. Larson (R-MN) asked John J. McSwain, "Does not the gentleman regard the children of the Nation as its most valuable resource?" the South Carolinian snorted, "Yes; but the children, if they are raised under a Prussianized system of submission to drill-sergeant methods of Federal control, will be of no value to America, I do not care how flushed their cheeks or how fat their forms." Ibid., p. 7190.

At least one congressman dished out a heaping portion of apple pie. Millard E. Tydings (of Maryland, natch) asked plaintively,

> Have we lost faith in the mothers of America—the mothers of the men who crossed the Alleghenies, settled the western prairies, and bore the boys who fought the Revolutionary, Civil, and World Wars? Shame on us. No greater insult could be hurled at womanhood, sitting in the sacredness of

her home, be it palace or thatched hovel, than to place over her these Federal agents.

Congressional Record, April 26, 1924, p. 7305.

102. *Congressional Record*, May 29, 1924, p. 9859. The *Woman Patriot* was partly subsidized by Senator James and Alice Hay Wadsworth, who had previously bankrolled the National Association Opposed to Woman Suffrage. Jane Jerome Camhi, "Women against Women: American Anti-Suffragism, 1880–1920" (Ph.D. diss., Tufts University, 1973), p. 156.

103. The extent to which both friends and foes of the child labor amendment saw it as being of a piece with its predecessor amendments is indicated by Montana senator Thomas Walsh, who dismissed Nicholas Murray Butler as "a stubborn reactionary, who has never become reconciled to the adoption of the eighteenth amendment, and who lent no aid to, if he did not actually oppose, both the sixteenth and the seventeenth." Quoted in Abbott, p. 553.

104. *Congressional Record*, May 29, 1924, p. 9863. An amendment to exempt agriculture failed 42 to 38. An amendment to reduce the age from eighteen to sixteen failed by 43–40; an attempt to slice the age to fourteen lost by 57 to 25.

105. The Michigan initiative to outlaw private schools lost on November 4, 1924, by a vote of 760,571 to 421,472.

106. Quoted in Sherman, p. 7.

107. *Congressional Record*, June 2, 1924, p. 10118.

108. James T. Patterson, *Mr. Republican* (Boston: Houghton Mifflin, 1972), p. 100.

109. Quoted in Trattner, p. 282.

110. Ibid., p. 150.

111. Ibid., p. 284.

112. House Document 497, p. 84.

113. *Congressional Record*, June 2, 1924, p. 10091.

114. Fuller, pp. 24–25.

115. *Congressional Record*, May 31, 1924, p. 9969.

116. Ibid., p. 9972. Maryland congressman John Philip Hull saw where all this was leading: "If you pass this Child Labor Amendment, you can not consistently refuse to pass a marriage and divorce amendment, placing under the charge of the Federal Government the closest and most fundamental relations of the home and of married life." *Congressional Record*, April 25, 1924, p. 7186. Bentley W. Warren made the same point in an influential essay, "Destroying Our 'Indestructible States,' " *Atlantic Monthly*, March 1924, pp. 370–78.

117. Charlotte Perkins Gilman, *The Home: Its Work and Influence* (New York: McClure, Phillips & Co., 1903), p. 313.

118. Ibid., pp. 59–60.

119. Ibid., p. 313.

120. Ibid., p. 335.

121. Quoted in W. A. Robinson, "Child Labor Amendment in Massachusetts," *American Political Science Review*, February 1925, p. 71.

122. Ibid.

123. Quoted in Lumpkin and Douglas, pp. 221, 232.

124. A political scientist, analyzing the Massachusetts vote, wrote in 1925: "Ever since the Civil War the tide has been running strongly toward federal centralization. Is it about to turn?" Nostradamus he wasn't. Robinson, p. 72.

125. Kelley's headstrong pursuit of plutocrat signatures backfired; she nearly bankrupted the National Consumers League. Josephine Goldmark, *Impatient Crusader* (Urbana: University of Illinois Press, 1953), pp. 118–19.

126. Quoted in Chambers, p. 45.

127. Fuller, p. 248. Even Albert Beveridge refused to support the amendment, writing that it threatened the "wholesome outdoor occupation of children." John Braeman, *Albert J. Beveridge: American Nationalist* (Chicago: University of Chicago Press, 1971), p. 300.

128. Trattner, p. 178.

129. Ibid., p. 193.

130. Ibid., p. 198.

131. Root had also been an active "wet," inspiring the witticism that Hires root beer had been renamed "Beer Hires Root."

132. Martin, p. 650.

133. Bromley, p. 132.

134. Quoted in Trattner, p. 204.

135. Abbott, p. 471.

136. *The Long Road: 40th Anniversary Report of the NCLC* (New York: National Child Labor Committee, 1944), p. 7.

137. Sherman, p. 15.

138. Quoted in Johnson, p. 188.

2

Weatherbeaten Shacks, Ignorant Parents: What's behind School Consolidation?

On March 2, 1991, the Wyoming Indians, the smallest basketball-playing school in New York State's Section 5, took the floor for the Class D championship in Rochester's cavernous War Memorial auditorium. Since the first point guard dribbled out of the primeval ooze Wyoming had dwelt in the basketball cellar: for years, 2–16 was regarded as a successful season. The team had never come anywhere near a sectional final before.

What made this game wrenchingly poignant was that it was also Wyoming High's swan song. The previous autumn Wyoming's taxpayers, burdened by the levies that are a direct consequence of state education mandates, voted 320 to 284 to close Wyoming's fifty-six-student high school after the 1990–1991 school year. The referendum was shot through with acrimony; many of the resultant ballot-scars will never heal.

Virtually all of Wyoming fit in one patch of the War Memorial. There were proud parents, craggy old-timers, and little brothers and sisters struck dumb by the size of the arena. Hand-scrawled banners bore such legends as "Wyoming High Will Never Die." But of course it would. The team won a thrilling game, 74–70. Neighbors embraced, the players and their townsmen cried without shame, and then it was over.[1]

Come the next fall, Wyoming's high-school-age students were "tuitioned out" to five other districts; most of the basketball team went to Alexander, ten miles away, reviving the fortunes of that perennial doormat and depriving Alexander residents of the pride of watching their own children play ball. (Is this what vouchers promise? Further destruction of the neighborhood school?)

The Batavia paper, one link in an absentee-owned chain, editorialized, "Wyoming is so small that it has fallen behind the times. As the world has become more complex, so too has education. The school could no longer offer the refinements that high schoolers need when they go out into the world."[2]

What this gibberish means is that Wyoming lacked a complement of computers, though by all accounts reading and writing and arithmetic were competently taught to the young scholars. But, as we shall see, the paper was humming a familiar tune: for the last century, rural parents have been told that sending their progeny to small nearby schools is a form of child abuse. Only large centralized education factories run by parchment collectors can produce a thoroughly modern kiddie: technology-literate, properly socialized, able and willing to serve as fodder in whatever wars (World, Cold, global economic) Uncle Sam is fighting this week.

Imagine ten thousand, twenty thousand, fifty thousand Wyomings, community schools blotted from existence either by state fiat or the bureaucratic equivalent of bribery. Imagine children whose short walk to the district school was replaced by long wagon or bus rides. Imagine parents rendered impotent in the administration of the unfamiliar schools to which their children were assigned. Imagine a countryside mottled by the relics John Greenleaf Whittier saw:

> Still sits the school-house by the road,
>   A ragged beggar sleeping;
> Around it still the sumachs grow,
>   And blackberry-vines are creeping.[3]

This is the sadness, the mindless destruction, that school consolidation wreaked—and still wreaks.

GETTING A RAZE

"The idea of consolidation seems to have originated in Massachusetts" in the mid-nineteenth century.[4] Horace Mann—was ever a suspect more usual?—disliked the "district" system by which parents financed and governed (sometimes even built) their own schools. Consolidation meant abolishing these tiny district academies and herding the students into much larger township schools. As Wayne E. Fuller documents in his superb social history *The Old Country School* (1982), consolidation transferred control of children's education from unlettered parents living on branch roads to professional educators enthroned in county seats (or, later, state capitals).[5]

"Parents," wrote the Nebraska superintendent of public instruction in 1873, "are often very poor judges of what a school should be."[6] A Michigan educator was just as frank in an 1879 speech:

The only way I see to better the condition of the [country] schools is to take just as much of their control out of the hands of the people as is possible. The people do not know the needs of the schools. They have been educated in these poor schools, and until the schools are better the people will be ignorant. . . . Centralization is what we need in school management.[7]

(Say this for the progressives of the late nineteenth and early twentieth centuries: they were honest men, and no matter how sinister their schemes may have been they never gussied them up in smiley-face euphemism.)

The national consolidation movement didn't really take off until the Progressive Moment at the dawn of our century. Big was deemed better than small, city better than country, and oligarchic rule by men with advanced degrees was better than a messy democracy in which the uneducated rabble had a voice.

With the arrogance and smug surety of those possessing arcane (if useless) knowledge, the professionals put forth as axiomatic claims later revealed to be flatly untrue. "Pupils have the advantage of that interest, enthusiasm, and confidence that large classes always bring," asserted William K. Fowler, Nebraska's superintendent of public instruction, in 1903.[8]

Harry A. Little of the Georgia State College for Women in Milledgeville (Flannery O'Connor's college; would that Little had wiser blood) averred that consolidation permitted "modern educational programs" to "be offered for the least possible amount of money."[9]

The scant research undergirding the consolidationist position was usually conducted under the auspices of universities, often state-supported.[10] A 1934 University of Kansas study found that "the number of excessive small school units is obviously unreasonable and needlessly expensive"[11]; a Columbia University scholar in that same year dismissively announced, "The small district with its small school belongs to a social order which has long been obsolete."[12]

Opponents, at least in the initial onslaught, were reduced to clinging to "bad roads" as their buoy, as administrators dismissed less practical objections—for instance, those growing from grass-roots democracy—as the fetid vaporings of inbred morons.

Any argument that was not quantifiable was null. For instance, no heft was assigned to sophisticated but unscientific essays such as that by Walter Sargent in *New England Magazine*. Sargent praised the rural district system because it "enforced and represented the conviction of the necessity of personal support for a vital object in the community's midst, and made it a habit. This habit of local support was the primal condition of the success of a common school system."[13] The district school, created and overseen by parents and neighbors, was autochthonous, unlike the alien contrivances of the professionals, which bore the same relationship to the local folk as the Viking lander did to Mars.

"Practically every objection [to consolidation] can be removed by proper administration," boasted Lee L. Driver, director of Pennyslvania's Bureau of Rural Education. The remaining naysayers were to be bulldozed. "Majorities are not always right and oftentimes the weight of an intelligent minority in a community should be considered rather than the majority of people," he told the National Education Association in 1922. "I like to think that the determining factor should be the majority of the intelligence of a community rather than a majority of number."[14]

But then a funny thing happened. The numbers and standardized tests so fetishized by the professional educators found little difference in the achievements of one-room and consolidated-school students. "Indeed," notes Fuller, "in the lower grades, one through six, the one-room schools were quite as good as the more costly consolidated schools, and with a lengthened school term might even have been superior."[15]

Facts, as our 40th president memorably remarked, are stupid things, and the consolidators were not deterred. In 1923, Adelaide S. Baylor, chairwoman of the U.S. Bureau of Education, instructed the National Education Association: "The conversion of the people through propaganda is essential to successful consolidation."[16] Her audience was listening; for years the *Journal of the National Education Association* featured accounts of progressive administrators vanquishing provincial mossbacks. A typical story, "A Banner Victory!," saluted the gleaming new $500,000 central school in Banner County, Nebraska, to which lucky students were bused from as far as thirty-five miles away.[17] (Today, teacher's unions are often shoulder-to-shoulder with parents in opposing consolidation.)

The popular press occasionally ran a wistful story about a doughty little schoolhouse on the lonesome prairie, but more often it served as a conduit for the agitprop of the modernizers. Journalist Benjamin Fine, in a series of articles for the *New York Times* later collected in *Our Children Are Cheated* (1947), visited several one and two-room schoolhouses— "unpainted, weatherbeaten, drab"[18]—and found sallow forlorn waifs "huddled in their overcoats"[19] and larnin' that the world is flat and the stork brings babies and the boogeyman'll getcha once the sun goes down. Compared to Fine's dilapidated shacks filled with cretins, Tobacco Road looked like Newport, Rhode Island.

"The rural schools are fifty years behind" the times, Fine estimated. "Many of these Rip Van Winkles are still sleeping soundly, unaware of new developments and changes that have taken place in education and the world at large."[20]

We'd have been better off listening to Larry Fine than Ben. Two decades later psychologists Roger Barker and Paul Gump indicted the centralizers as the real cheaters of our children: "What size should a school
be? The data of this research and our own educational values tell us that
a school should be sufficiently small that all of its students are needed for
all of its enterprises. A school should be small enough that its students
are not redundant."[21]

Voluminous anecdotal—that is, personal and meaningful—evidence
testifies to the enriching nature of human-scale education. While Benjamin Fine was exposing himself to the horror-show of rural America, San-
dra Baker Kauffman, my mother, was attending the one-room (made two
by a partition) schoolhouse in the hamlet of Lime Rock, New York, at
least until she and her classmates were transferred—over the vigorous if
nugatory objections of their parents—to Le Roy Central School. Her
memories of the Lime Rock school are warm and pleasing. Le Roy, by con-
trast, was "terrifying" in its bigness; and she had learned Le Roy's fifth-
grade lessons in Lime Rock's fourth grade. Of course she adapted, as
most students do when their school is closed, but Lime Rock suffered a
loss from which it never recovered.

Of the three community institutions that gave Lime Rock its identity—the school, the town baseball team, and St. Anthony's Roman
Catholic church—only the third survives. The older folks recall, with
hearty laughs and significant quavers, the Christmas plays and the out-
house and the lore of the school, just as they have retold into legend the
apical event of Lime Rock's history: its defeat of hated Le Roy in an epic
baseball game, and the all-night horn-blowing raucous celebration that
followed. But the young people of today's Lime Rock, who board the bus
for the long ride to Le Roy every morn, will never know that kind of pride.
The school is gone, high grass obscures the ballfield, and one wonders
how much longer tiny Lime Rock will exist in anything but memory.
Snuffed—and for what?[22]

Ask a resident of one of the many towns that fell victim to consolidation how keenly she feels the school's absence. These villages have lost
not only a gathering place but also an essential transmitter of local memory, local awareness, and local history. Wendell Berry has written in opposition to Bigness in Education:

There must be love of learning and of the cultural tradition and of
excellence—and this love cannot exist, because it makes no sense,
apart from the love of a place and a community. Without this love,
education is only the importation into a local community of cen-
trally prescribed "career preparation" designed to facilitate the ex-
port of young careerists.[23]

Benjamin Fine had an answer for ole Wendell. "We are a nation of nomads. Millions of men and women cross state borders as readily as one visits his neighbor across the street. For that reason, education is no longer solely a state responsibility."[24] (The notion that it was a local or even parental responsibility was by now so ancient as to be beneath mention.)

Still, there were holdouts, and new carrots and sticks had to be grown and sharpened. Adelaide S. Baylor urged "bonus[es] offered for consolidated schools": after all, didn't everyone have his price?[25] In any event, the Second World War was taking care of part of the problem: the war caused a severe teacher shortage; and as rural instructors moved to fill positions in the cities, consolidation was forced, willy-nilly, upon some schools. But this was not all the Good War was to give us.

CONANT THE BARBARIAN

By midcentury, as the U.S. government settled into what now seems to be a permanent mobilization for war, community-run rural schools had become more than quaint anachronisms—they were a peril to our very existence. The high priest of Cold War consolidation was James Bryant Conant, the chemist and Harvard University president who had been a major in the Army's Chemical Warfare Service during the First World War and a Manhattan Project administrator during the second.

After devoting the best years of his life to devising ever more horrific methods of slaughtering people he'd never met, Dr. Conant turned his attentions upon America's schoolchildren. With a grant from the Carnegie Corporation, he produced a series of scowling reports on the state of American education.

Conant's most controversial recommendation was for "the elimination of the small high school."[26] Without bothering to adduce evidence, Conant declared that no graduating class of fewer than one hundred students ought to be tolerated.

Why? Russia's fault, of course. Those who resisted centralization were "still living in imagination in a world which knew neither nuclear weapons nor Soviet imperialism. They believe they can live and prosper in an isolated, insulated United States."[27] Conant disparaged those sentimentalists who "resent any references to the struggle between the free nations and Communism and the consequent existence of a special national interest which ought to affect educational planning."[28]

Believe it or not, Conant marveled, in the mist-shrouded past

[The state] was remarkably indifferent as to whether parents chose to take advantage of the educational opportunities offered, and local authorities sometimes were not very strict in enforcing the com-

pulsory attendance laws. . . . As long as the public concern was
directed almost exclusively to the education of future voters and
the unfolding of the personality of each child, a thousand very different schools might be considered an excellent idea.[29]

But then along came Germany, then Russia, then China, then North Ko-
rea, and Washington developed "an overriding state interest" in molding
children into the soldiers and engineers and atomic-bomb designers of
the brave new world.

(The Cold War was used as an excuse for countless programs that disrupted normal American life and overturned the federal system, from
the National Defense Education Act to the Interstate and Defense Highway system. If you wanted to pass an obnoxious or expensive piece of legislation in the 1950s, you just inserted "Defense" into the title.)

"Not many years ago," Conant wrote, "a considerable body of opinion
in this country . . . thought that what happened to children was a matter
for the parents to decide. The state should not come between a father and
his son. . . . These arguments would sound archaic today."[30]

And this, really, is the fundament of the Conant view. The child belongs to the state, not to the parent: he is a little soldier in a thirteen-year
boot camp who will, if necessary, be bused twenty, thirty, even fifty miles
to gleaming, soulless, ostensibly hyper-efficient superschools, where he
can be programmed to be a "productive worker" who can "meet the challenges of the Soviet menace/the space race/the twenty-first century"—fill in the blank. He is a cog, a drone, a spoke—all in all he's just
another brick in the wall.

The fewer the schools and the more uniform their curricula, the easier
it would be to create the Cold War American youth. Russell Kirk knew
this. In 1958 he wrote that the "abolition of rural schools" was aimed at
"breaking down regional and vocational distinctions and producing 'int-
egrated' Americans."[31]

Private schools were off the hook due to that pettifogging Constitution, but Conant—a product of Roxbury Latin and Harvard—warned
that the "greater the proportion of our youth who fail to attend public
schools and who receive their education elsewhere, the greater the
threat to democratic unity."[32] (This was foreseen long ago by Henry Adams, who wrote in his autobiography: "All State education is a sort of dy-
namo machine for polarizing the popular mind; for turning and holding
its lines of force in the direction supposed to be most effective for state
purposes."[33])

One problem tested Conant. How to wipe out tens of thousands of
small schools? Public opinion ruled out the use of his favorite weapons on
the country cousins, so he blandly recommended: "Imaginative leadership is necessary at the state level in order to promote the necessary local

action."[34] What he meant by this was spelled out elsewhere in a footnote: "compulsory measures . . . without recourse to popular vote."[35] (Note the perverse use of "imaginative" as a synonym for "tyrannical.")

Conant was in no mood to hear a lot of guff about long bus rides or attachments to the old home town. "Geography may sometimes be legitimate justification for a small high school, but all too often it is merely an excuse. Human nature—not geography—offers the real explanation."[36] By "human nature" Conant apparently meant such immeasurables as love, kinship, loyalty, and ancestral memory, factors that had no place in his equations.

Unfortunately, huge expanses of this spacious country are sparsely populated; unless the tykes take the Concorde to school, a class of one hundred cannot be mustered. For these deprived anchorites Conant suggested state subsidies "to enable students to board at schools of sufficient size from Monday through Thursday."[37] Smaller schools were to be wiped out—by any means necessary. Thus would the state separate child and parent and force rural families to ape the practice of the ruling class, whose adolescents are warehoused in distant prep academies. Behold the little Andover on the prairie.

The corporate media loved Conant. He was the country's "educational statesman," fawned the *Saturday Review*.[38] He was lionized in *Time*, which complained: "Compared to Europe's state-run systems, U.S. schools seem an anarchist's brainchild."[39] But not to worry, *Time*: though Conant groused that of all his recommendations consolidation was "the one most vigorously attacked," it proceeded apace.[40]

THE BEATING GOES ON

The number of school districts in America has free fallen: 127,531 in 1932; 83,718 in 1950; 40,520 in 1960; 17,995 in 1970; 15,709 in 1980; 14,556 in 1992. Admittedly, urbanization did in some of the rural districts, but population growth and tenacious decentralism could have checked the decline.

Does it matter that every promise of the consolidationists has been shown up as at best an exaggeration, at worst a lie? For one thing, "Transportation costs, typically overlooked by zealous consolidators, add substantially to the costs of larger districts farther away from student's homes," writes education researcher Toni Haas. "If a price were attached to the time students spend on buses, cost savings in larger rural districts decline substantially."[41]

Moreover, a growing, by now impressively stout body of evidence indicates that small schools—"those enrolling no more than 400 students in high school, for instance"—"may provide better educations than their larger counterparts, as a function (at least in part) of their small size."[42]

This is a choice number, 400: these schools, often the very best, were precisely the ones James Conant wished to kill.

I do not use "kill" carelessly. School buildings, as Alan Peshkin understands, cannot be razed without consequence. For each is "a graphic reminder of an often hallowed past . . . the physical embodiment of old friendships, old fun, old contests, and, as well, an old self."[43]

Or as Wayne E. Fuller puts it:

> To close a country school was to destroy an institution that held the little rural community together. It was to wipe out the one building the people of the district had in common and, in fact, to destroy the community, which, in those years, so many were trying to save and strengthen. Even more important, as far as the farmers were concerned, the destruction of their school meant that their power to set the length of the school terms, to employ their teacher, and to determine how much they would spend for education would be taken from them and given to some board far removed from their community and their control.[44]

Yet even at this late date, all is not lost—else the consolidators would not still be at it. James Conant has been dead for nigh twenty years, but there's more where he came from. The rationale for consolidation has changed. The Soviet bugbear has been replaced by the global economy. And as Alan Peshkin notes, "the twin demons of inflation and plummeting enrollments" are often advertised as the pure motivations of Conant's spawn.[45] The new consolidators sometimes pose as the taxpayer's friend, diligently sniffing out wasteful spending (although, like the consolidators of old, they almost invariably call for increased federal aid to education: skinflints they're not).

One of the most recent bitter battles occurred in New York, when in May 1992 Governor Cuomo's commissioner of education, Thomas Sobol, of the wealthy suburb of Scarsdale, ordered his subalterns to determine how best to undertake a program of mass consolidation which would leave no school district in the state with fewer than 1,200 pupils. (This would've meant abolishing 292 of the state's 718 districts.)

By November, Sobol had refined his proposal: he requested the power to close or merge school districts that did not meet any one of a set of five arbitrary criteria. (This hit list contained 139 districts.) Sobol had Conant's distaste for "geography as excuse," though he did allow that travel time should not exceed ninety minutes for 7th through 12th graders and an hour for younger students. (High-school-less Wyoming was placed on the list because it had "a grade organization other than kindergarten through 12th grade." You take the carrot, and then, too late, find that it was poisonous.)

"We are running a $21 billion enterprise. We want to be sure we are doing so efficiently," said Sobol, and in parsing the sentence almost every significant word or phrase—"we are running" and "billion" and "efficiently"—bespeaks the malignant nature of mass education.[46]

Sobol backed down in the face of protest from small districts and the New York State United Teachers. "It's a crown of thorns, not any other kind of crown," pled Sobol (whom few had ever accused of being Christlike) in response to charges that he sought to make himself king.[47]

Sobol and Cuomo are gone, but New York continues to offer thirty pieces of silver—known as "financial incentives"—to districts that close schools. The most effective way to bludgeon rural folks into selling out their birthright is to mandate a curriculum—a minimum of three foreign languages, an advanced placement course in computer science—so expensive that hard-pressed taxpayers will vote for the false "economy" promised by the centralizers.

New York and other states gladly fund "studies" by education consultants of the benefits and drawbacks—guess which always outweighs the other?—of merger. A recent effort to bribe the arch-rival New York townships of Le Roy and Pavilion into combining was voted down by a huge margin, much to the dismay of the Gannett chain newspaper in Rochester, whose editorialists lectured that "communities must suspend feelings of loyalty."[48]

The fault line in this debate doesn't necessarily run along the urban-rural divide. In New York, one of the most articulate champions of human-scale schooling was Deborah Meier, former codirector of the acclaimed Central Park East public school in East Harlem. "In schools," Meier writes, "big doesn't work no matter how one slices the data. Large schools neither nourish the spirit nor educate the mind; except for a small elite who run the place and claim (falsely) to know everyone, what big schools do is remind most of us that we don't count for a lot."[49]

Community schools are possible in "stable urban neighborhoods," Alan Peshkin asserted in *The Imperfect Union* (1984), his thorough account of an Illinois village's fight to save its grade school from death by consolidation. But they exist "most notably in small, homogeneous places," and these are the places that have been ground zero for the Conants of every generation.[50]

As one father of four argued during the New York controversy: "The stereotype that our small schools are quaint, rustic, and preserved only out of a sense of nostalgia fails to recognize that our small rural school districts are breathing organs of real communities—communities that are entitled to their own culture, values and local control. Rural people deserve the same respect that the multiculturalists insist on for urban and immigrant minorities."[51]

In the late 1970s, a new-wave band with the wonderfully apposite name (for purposes of this chapter) Student Teachers sang, "I see what this is leading to—and it looks real grim." Where does the logic of consolidation lead us? To a land of empty Wyoming Highs, longer school days, a national curriculum drawn up in Washington, no more summer vacations, and other nostrums intended to Nipponize (the verb used to be "Prussianize") American children. (Again, the much-maligned teacher's unions are the primary foes of these schemes.) The job of the parents is to buy the tykes computers on which to play video games: beyond that, Mom and Dad, get lost!

Los Angeles mayor Tom Bradley gave us a glimpse of one possible grim future when, in 1985, he proposed that feckless parents who weren't up to the task of prepping little Jamal or LaTisha for the challenge of twenty-first-century burger flipping cede them to the Los Angeles school district. "I would propose that we take them as early as we can get them in elementary school and keep them in that school setting, that formalized training and motivational setting, away from their parents, because that's what it's going to take."

Bradley saw twenty-four-hour schooling as a simple extension of "child-care centers. It's the same concept. Simply you would extend that child-care treatment . . . for enough time that those youngsters are not going to be exposed to their home environment where they are destined to fail."[52]

The consolidation debate was never really about optimum classroom size. The nub of the issue was bared by a writer in the *Canadian Forum* in 1938: "The greatest problem facing Canadian public education is the problem of the small financial unit."[53] Substitute "human" for "financial" and you've hit the mark. The real problem was the small human unit, the child, who was to be folded, spindled, and mutilated by the state and by professionals who know everything a parent does not need to know.

ONWARD TO . . . WHAT?

Each town has its own story, blessed with a uniqueness wrought by decades of natural and human action. When you kill a school something in that town dies, and it can never be resurrected.

In 1950 *Life* magazine reported, with requisite sneering, on the war between Onward and Walton, small towns located five miles apart in Cass County, Indiana: "The two towns have always maintained separate schools and a bitter sports rivalry, exhibiting in an intense way the exaggerated chauvinism with which American parents regard their school and their home-town basketball teams."

When, at the behest of the state legislature, Walton school trustee Virgil Turner tried to force a merger—Onward would get the grade school,

Walton the high school—a ruction broke out (at what *Life* called the "lunatic local level"):

> When school started on Sept. 5, Walton grade school children came over to Onward without any fuss, but Onward high school students, except for nine apostates, stayed away from Walton. When Onward parents heard that Turner was planning to take their high school furniture off to Walton in a truck, they recruited a defense brigade and dared him to try. They guarded the school 24 hours a day, manned a portable air-raid siren and scouted the road to Walton with a small plane. Argument and vituperation flew between the towns. Said Onward Truck Driver Edgar Grant, "There's too much delinquency over there. Walton children run all over the streets and the poolrooms at Kokomo." Farmer Calvin Albers, a leader of the Onward group, said he thought the Walton children lacked moral training. "There are no vulgar poems or markings on the toilets at Onward," he observed pointedly. Mrs. Russell Price said, "Walton isn't qualified to run a high school." Retorted Trustee Turner, "The people at Onward just don't want to lose their basketball team."
>
> The pot came to a boil on Oct. 6. That morning Turner rented a dump truck for $1 and recruited 15 Walton volunteers, one of whom, a bartender, promptly fainted from excitement. They loaded up the Walton elementary school desks and headed for Onward to exchange them for Onward high school equipment. But an Onward agent in Walton sent a warning. A tootling of horns sounded the alarm, and when the truck drove in 50 grim-faced Onward citizens manned the high school battlements and surrounded the Waltonites. A few punches were thrown. Then the Waltonites retreated to inform Turner that the invasion had failed. Meanwhile Onward students attended their own "rebel" high school, with three teachers paid by local subscription. It looked as if the state would have to step in.[54]

And Onward got stepped on. One eyewitness to the fracas, Robert E. Montgomery, a retired teacher-administrator from Young America, Indiana, remembers seeing "women standing in the doorways with pitchforks and hoes and rakes." But these weapons were not enough to slay the dragon Progress, at least not this time, and the kids from Onward wound up being "bused all over the place," according to Montgomery.[55]

Life found the whole episode an amusing case in local color, though to the men, women, and children of Onward something was at stake far beyond the understanding of Henry Luce. To those who believe in our America, Onward is a Gettysburg, a Selma, a Waco—the stuff of which myths are made.

Shall Onward be forgotten? Or shall Onward be avenged? How many more Onwards must there be?

NOTES

1. No article on Wyoming's wondrous season was complete without reference to *Hoosiers*, a beautiful 1986 film about the ways in which a successful high school basketball team enriches a small Indiana town in the 1950s. In one piercingly ironic scene, a student recites the glories of "progress": electricity, indoor plumbing, and school consolidation. This third wonder of the modern age will soon swallow up thousands of the little schools whose praises *Hoosiers* so movingly sings.

2. "Wyoming Team a Thriller," Batavia *Daily News*, March 9, 1991, p. 4.

3. John Greenleaf Whittier, "In School-Days," *The Complete Poetical Works of Whittier* (Boston: Houghton Mifflin, 1894), p. 407.

4. Lee L. Driver, "The Consolidation of Rural Schools," *Addresses and Proceedings of the National Education Association*, 1922, p. 1209.

5. I cannot overpraise Fuller's marvelous book. Read it for yourself, then send it to your favorite teacher or an educable educator. Wayne E. Fuller, *The Old Country School* (Chicago: University of Chicago, 1982).

6. Fuller, p. 107.

7. Ibid., p. 113.

8. William K. Fowler, "Consolidation of Rural Schools," *Addresses and Proceedings of the National Education Association*, 1903, p. 921. Not all fervent consolidationists were unmindful of the harmful consequences of their actions. In 1915, L. H. Bailey urged "putting into the rural districts at least one institution or enterprise for every one that is taken out." Why take one out in the first place? Why kill what is organic and replace it with the artificial? L. H. Bailey, "A Danger in Rural School Consolidation," *School and Society*, February 27, 1915, p. 316.

9. Harry A. Little, *School and Society*, October 20, 1934, p. 527.

10. For instance, Ohio State University, the University of Texas, the University of Indiana, and the University of Oklahoma. Harry A. Little, *Potential Economies in the Reorganization of Local School Attendance Units* (New York: Columbia University, 1934), p. 8.

11. F. P. O'Brien, "Economies Possible in Larger School Units," *Kansas Studies in Education*, 2, no. 3 (June 1934): 6–7.

12. Harry A. Little, *Potential Economies*, p. 5.

13. Walter Sargent, "The Passing of the Old Red Schoolhouse," *New England Magazine* 23 (December 1900): 424.

14. Driver, pp. 1209–10.

15. Fuller, p. 243.

16. Adelaide S. Baylor, "Consolidation of Rural Schools," *Addresses and Proceedings of the National Education Association*, 1923, p. 295.

17. "A Banner Victory!" *Journal of the National Education Association* 50 (May 1961): 51–52.

18. Benjamin Fine, *Our Children Are Cheated* (New York: Holt, 1947), p. 139.

19. Ibid., p. 133.

20. Ibid., p. 142.

21. Quoted in Alan Peshkin, *The Imperfect Union* (Chicago: University of Chicago, 1982), p. 162.

22. Chat with my mother at the Miss Batavia Diner, December 1, 1995.

23. Wendell Berry, "The Work of Local Culture," in *What Are People For?* (San Francisco: North Point, 1990), p. 164.

24. Fine, p. 229.

25. Baylor, p. 295.

26. James Bryant Conant, *The American High School Today* (New York: McGraw-Hill, 1959), p. 38.

27. James Bryant Conant, *The Child, the Parent, and the State* (Cambridge, Mass.: Harvard University Press, 1959), p. 39. One of Conant's other totalitarian enthusiasms was universal military training. See James Hershberg, *James B. Conant* (New York: Knopf, 1993), p. 310.

28. Conant, *The Child, the Parent, and the State*, p. 39. One of the Cold War era's rare, non-elegiac defenses of the one-room school appeared in the *Saturday Evening Post* by Grant McConnell, a political scientist (and author of *The Decline of Agrarian Democracy*) whose children attended a log cabin school in Stehekin, Washington. "Education is something we have had to build from the ground up," wrote McConnell. "[Our daughter] knows that we are interested, because we went to the last work day and helped paint the ceiling. If parents are troubled by what is going on, they have lots of chances for casual talk with the teacher." Grant McConnell, "There's a Case for at Least One Single-Room Schoolhouse," *Saturday Evening Post*, March 3, 1956, p. 12.

29. Conant, *The Child, the Parent, and the State*, p. 17.

30. Ibid., p. 13.

31. Russell Kirk, "Rural Schools: Are They Worth Keeping?" *American Mercury*, March 1958, p. 68. Kirk also wrote: "Local control of schools, and location of schools within each distinct community, is in keeping with our free and democratic American society, while centralization of the school-system tends to take authority away from parents and communities." "Rural Schools," p. 69.

32. "James Bryant Conant—Educational Statesman," *Saturday Review*, October 15, 1960, p. 89.

33. Henry Adams, *The Education of Henry Adams* (New York: Modern Library, 1946 [1918]), p. 78.

34. Conant, *The American High School Today*, p. 82.

35. Conant, *The Child, the Parent, and the State*, p. 174.

36. Conant, *The American High School Today*, p. 84.

37. Conant, *The Child, the Parent, and the State*, p. 173.

38. "James Bryant Conant—Educational Statesman," *Saturday Review*, October 15, 1960, p. 88.

39. "The Inspector General," *Time*, September 14, 1959, p. 70.

40. Quoted in Robert Hampel, *The Last Little Citadel* (Boston: Houghton Mifflin, 1986), p. 70.

41. Toni Haas, "Why Reform Doesn't Apply: Creating a New Story about Education in Rural America," in *Rural Education: Issues and Practice*, ed. Alan J. DeYoung (New York: Garland, 1991), p. 428.

42. Ibid., p. 430.

43. Peshkin, p. 160. What former California Governor Jerry Brown said of the closing of churches in San Francisco is as true of schools:

> A church is a repository of shared experience, of suffering, of initiation—from baptism to marriage to death—and all those memories consecrate a building and make it a shrine that cannot summarily be traded for money. . . . The idea of merging parishes is an abomination. What does that mean, merge churches? Their separate identities have been won out of 150 years of experience. You just kill it, that's all.

"Jerry Brown Talks," *Chronicles*, November 1994, p. 20.

44. Fuller, pp. 234–35.

45. Peshkin, p. 6.

46. Doris Wolf and Billy House, "A Mergers Wish-List Hits Home," Rochester *Democrat and Chronicle*, December 18, 1992, p. A1.

47. Billy House, "Forced School Merger Plan Proves Divisive," Rochester *Democrat and Chronicle*, December 19, 1992, p. A1.

48. "The Urging of Merger," Rochester *Democrat and Chronicle*, May 13, 1992, editorial page.

49. Deborah Meier, *The Power of Their Ideas* (Boston: Beacon, 1995), p. 107.

50. Peshkin, p. 164.

51. Stephen Walker, "Headline Missed Point," Rochester *Democrat and Chronicle*, December 24, 1992, letters.

52. "What the Mayor Actually Said," *Los Angeles Herald-Examiner*, August 15, 1985, p. A10.

53. "Little School House in the Red," *Canadian Forum*, February 1938, p. 379.

54. "Little Onward Won't Be Moved," *Life*, October 16, 1950, pp. 48–49. And what's wrong with not wanting to lose a basketball team? In an interview, Penn State football coach Joe Paterno told me that school consolidation is to blame for the decline of Western Pennsylvania high school football: "What happened was a lot of the little coal towns joined together as one school. Where you used to have five schools with maybe 60 kids each out for football—300 kids—now you might have one joint school with 50 kids out." "Live with TAE: Joe Paterno," *American Enterprise*, November/December 1996, p. 21.

55. Phone conversation with Robert E. Montgomery, December 20, 1995. Montgomery is a member of the school board of Southeastern School Corporation, the district into which Onward and Walton and others have since been folded. Where once there were fifteen area high schools, says Montgomery, now there are only three. He reports that forty-five years after the closing, there are still hard feelings in Onward.

3

Who in Her Right Mind Opposed Woman Suffrage?

Old Father Hubbard,
Went to the cupboard,
To get his poor children some bread;
Mother 'Suffrage,' the sinner,
Had forgotten their dinner,
So they had to go hungry to bed.

—Anti-suffrage nursery rhyme[1]

How strangely the cause of anti-suffragism strikes us today. What knuckle-dragging brute could possibly oppose votes for women? And the women among their legion—Antis, as they were known—what was the source of their derangement? Were they timid church mice? Or self-abnegating ciphers, foregoing the ballot and immolating themselves in the flames of the eternal kitchen fire?

Like all losers in political contests, the Antis have gotten a bad historiographical press. "One might assume that antifeminism or antisuffragism in women was a form of psychopathology," ventured one historian, typically.[2] (An exception is Manuela Thurner, who is discussed in an endnote.)[3]

The Antis did put forth their share of silly and hysterically expressed reasons why the polling place should remain stag. A favorite of mine was the fear that tens of thousands of prostitutes would sell their votes; but how were the Antis to know that years later, the prostitutes would be asking *us* for *our* votes?

It is a measure of the bog into which our polity has sunk that the whole matter now seems supremely silly, much ado about an inconsequential depression of a lever. Anti Molly Elliot Seawell, a Virginia novelist and descendant of President John Tyler, fretted,

> Political differences in families . . . do not promote harmony. How much more inharmonious must be political differences between a husband and wife, each of whom has a vote which may be used as a weapon against the other? What is likely to be the state of that family, when the husband votes one ticket, and the wife votes another?[4]

Good golly Miss Molly: in the glare of hindsight, this concern is absurd! The ballot today is virtually meaningless. Quarrels between husbands and wives over the merits, so to speak, of Clinton and Dole were liable to be far less vehement than an argument over whether to buy Coke or Pepsi.[5]

Yet the Antis asked impertinent questions and raised venerable banners. If their immediate object—abjuring the ballot—was a lost and not (to the author, at least) particularly praiseworthy cause, natheless the ground they stood is a part of our heritage that is worth preserving. They deserve our attention and respect.[6]

(ANTI)SUFFRAGETTE CITY

Woman suffrage came first to the mountain states. Wyoming legislators thought it a good way to advertise the territory to prospective settlers; in Utah, it endowed polygamous families with extra votes and demonstrated to a disapproving East that women, if given the chance, would not vote to abolish this peculiar institution. (Mormon-baiting was a staple of Anti-literature. Molly Elliot Seawell sniffed, "While, happily, all suffragists are not Mormons, all Mormons are suffragists.")[7]

To derail the suffrage bandwagon, potent Anti organizations arose in more than twenty-five states; a National Association Opposed to Woman Suffrage (NAOWS) was founded in New York City in 1911. New York and Massachusetts were hotbeds of Anti agitation, and as a result the extant literature is probably unrepresentative of Antis as a whole. There is a Victorian fustiness about the old pamphlets; too much Boston, not enough Kansas.

But the suffragists hissed that it was a fraud anyway: Anna Howard Shaw, a Methodist minister and president of the National American Woman Suffrage Association (NAWSA), scoffed of the Antis: "They are just enough in number so that by holding out their skirts they can make a screen for the men operating dens of vice and iniquity and prostitution to hide behind."[8]

This was a lie, as even unsympathetic historians grant: the remarkable thing about the American opposition to woman suffrage is that, except for a few old fogies like Lyman Abbott and Francis Parkman, the movement was a female production.

The Antis had no single creed; there was a crazy-quilt quality about them. At their best, they were a beguiling blend of traditionalist and anarchist: "in the inner circle rules the woman," as Ida Tarbell put it, and where else would anyone wish to be?[9]

The worst of the lot were flag-waving viragoes who made craven attacks on Fola La Follette, Jane Addams, Jeannette Rankin, and other suffragists who courageously spoke out against Mr. Wilson's War. Then there were the Boston Brahmins who dripped anti-Catholicism: the thought of the Irish maid or bohunk washerwoman standing on equal political footing with Cabots and Lodges was cause for horripilation. (As Francis Parkman of the men's auxiliary wrote, Catholic immigrant women were "almost devoid of a sense of responsibility." But credit him for one good line. He feared that lady pols would "use their wiles" to get their way, though "if—and the contingency is in the highest degree probable—she is not gifted with charms of her own," she will procure proxy doxies. For "Delilah has already spread her snares for the congressional Sampson.")[10]

Molly Seawell emphasized that her disposition against suffrage was "not, in the smallest degree, based upon the assumption that women are not equal to men, but merely that men and women are not identical."[11] The difference was calculated by Mrs. Alice N. George, a Brookline, Massachusetts, Anti: "The sexes do not stand in the position of master and slave, of tyrant and victim. In a healthy state of society there is no rivalry between men and women; they were created different, and in the economy of life have different duties, but their interests are the common interests of humanity." The question was not equality, insisted Mrs. George, but rather shall women enter "the department of government or . . . the equally essential departments of education, society, and religion?" If the first, the upheaval will "strike at the family as the self-governing unit upon which the state is built."[12]

This traditionalist view—stated less often than you'd expect—was advanced by Massachusetts Anti Ruth Whitney Lyman:

The fundamental difference is this—that the suffragist (like the socialist) persists in regarding the individual as the unit of society, while the anti-suffragist insists that it is the family. . . . Anti-suffrage is founded upon the conception of co-operation between the sexes. Men and women must be regarded as partners, not competitors; and the family, to be preserved as a unit, must be represented by having one political head.[13]

Mrs. Lyman and her sisters denied that this guaranteed a tyranny of the male animal. After all, wrote Anne Hathaway Gulick, woman "already has every opportunity in her own special province to mold public opinion by educating the inmates of her home to live right and to think right."[14]

The distinction between state and society was sharpened by the redoubtable Ruth Whitney Lyman, for my money the keenest of the Massachusetts Antis. Wrote Mrs. Lyman,

> Suffragism stakes its faith on more government . . . upon control by law. The anti-suffragist sees the evils of society as fundamentally resulting from the evil in individuals, and calls on women to check it at its source. They emphasize the power of individual homes to turn out men and women who, trained to self-control, will not necessitate control by law. Knowing that the great training school for private morality is family life, the anti-suffragist seeks to preserve conditions making for sound family life, the sum total of private morality being public morality, the conscience of the people.[15]

Or as the Radcliffe scholar Elizabeth Jackson put it, "An essential weakness in the suffrage argument is the failure to distinguish between government and culture." The former is based on "compulsion" and awash in "selfishness, cruelty, and hate"; the latter comprises "the home, the church, the newspaper, and the public school." Because women rule the home and the primary school, "From women rather than men, our children learn the elements of good citizenship."[16]

This is all well and good, but what harm could adding the ballot to woman's arsenal possibly do?

Jeannette Gilder, literary editor of the *New York Herald*, answered in *Harper's Bazaar*: "[Give a] woman everything she wants, but not the ballot. Open every field of learning, every avenue of industry to her, but keep her out of politics. The ballot cannot help her, but it can hurt her. She thinks it is a simple piece of paper, but it is a bomb."[17]

Its first casualty would be woman's unassailable perch in public discourse: she'd be blasted out of her putatively disinterested, objective, and above-the-fray aerie. Mrs. Francis M. Scott, a New York Anti, explained: "The fact that women have no political prizes to gain, no offices in view, no constituencies to please, has made them of special value in [educational, municipal and charitable work]. . . . Let them be plunged into the arena of political strife and there will be no one left to carry on the work they now sustain so bravely."[18]

The special regard in which the political opinions of civic-minded women were held was a function of their distance from politics: when Dorothea Dix spoke before a legislative committee, the members listened (and frequently did what she asked); but attach a party label to Miss Dix and she'd have been just another hackette, grinding axes and playing the angles. "Let [men] struggle with the vote," said Emily Bissell, president of the Consumers' League of Delaware, who dismissed the ballot as a "clumsy male expedient. . . . Let us aim at legislation."[19]

H. L. Mencken, who was later to marry a suffragist, concurred. He said of women who joined the Democrats and Republicans: "A woman who joins one of these parties simply becomes an imitation man, which is to say, a donkey. Thereafter she is nothing but an obscure cog in an ancient and creaking machine, the sole intelligible purpose of which is to maintain a horde of scoundrels in public office."[20]

Novelist Annie Nathan Meyer, in the *North American Review*, assayed the soul-draining effect of becoming an apparat-chick: "It is so easy to be noble, to be generous, to be unselfish, on the public platform,—in one's typewritten Confession of Faith. How is the strength to be given to work on, to fight on quietly, unknown, uninterviewed, unrewarded, certainly unapplauded?" In a passage that ought to be drilled into the head of any politician or propagandist who utters the cant phrase "family values," Mrs. Meyer continued: "It is so easy to appeal on the platform to the highest, purest motives, to implore others to do their duty, and in the home to shrink from the most elementary duties, not only of motherhood, but of wifehood. It is so easy to be suave and delightful, gracious and charming, on the platform, and at home nervous, unstrung, impatient, fretful."[21]

Mrs. Meyer, a prominent New Yorker and a founder of Barnard College, had seen political men who posed as champions of the working class yet mistreated servants and employees; lovers of the human race who never seemed to get around to treating its constituent parts with respect. Why, she wondered, should women subject themselves to the degrading temptation of state power?

"Women don't change politics as much as politics changes women,"[22] said one Coloradan; to which a suffragist songster replied:

> It doesn't unsex her to toil in a factory
> Minding the looms from dawn until night;
> To deal with a schoolful of children refractory
> Doesn't unsex her in anyone's sight;
> Work in a store when her back aches unhumanly—
> Doesn't unsex her at all you will note,
> But think how exceedingly rough and unwomanly
> Woman would be if she happened to vote.[23]

She had a point—sort of. For the Antis were an exotic blend, and some of them did deplore the de-domesticating impact of the industrial revolution.[24] (As for "unsexing," Mencken cracked: "Perhaps a majority of the more ardent suffragists belonged biologically to neither sex."[25])

FOR WHOM THE TARBELLS?

Among the most complex of the anti-industrial Antis was Ida Tarbell, doyenne of the muckrakers.

The Antis were a lively mixture of reaction and radicalism, and so it is no surprise to find the ranks filled with women of letters. (The best writers of both sexes have often been half revolutionary, half stick-in-the-mud.) *Popular Science Monthly* editorialized, "One of the grievances of the suffrage leaders lay in the fact that the literary women of the country would express no sympathy with their efforts."[26] In earlier years these obscurants included Gail Hamilton, Harriet Beecher Stowe, and Catherine Beecher; throughout the teens their numbers included not only Mesdames Seawell, Gilder, and Meyer, but also Octave Thanet, a.k.a. Alice French, the highly praised realist short-story writer from Davenport, Iowa. But the woman whose support Antis prized above all others was the archetypal career woman, Ida Tarbell.

Ida Tarbell's father, an independent oilman from Titusville, Pennsylvania, exhausted himself in battles against John D. Rockefeller's Standard Oil monopoly. Ida was very much her father's daughter; her landmark *McClure's* series on the crimes and depredations of Standard Oil was about the nicest gift a girl could ever give dear old dad.

Tarbell eschewed direct political action: she shocked Washington by turning down President Wilson's proferred nomination to the Tariff Commission in 1916. But she did join the executive board of the New York State Association Opposed to the Extension of Suffrage to Women, and in a curious volume titled *The Business of Being a Woman* (1912) she explained herself—in a way.

She begins by paying tribute to the feminists she had revered in her youth:

> Certainly no woman who to-day takes it as a matter of course that she should study what she chooses, go and come as she will, support herself unquestioned by trade, profession, or art, work in public or private, handle her own property, share her children on equal terms with her husband, receive a respectful attention on platform or before legislature, live freely in the world, should think with anything but reverence particularly of the early disturbers of convention and peace [at Seneca Falls in 1848].[27]

(Though she did note that the feminists of the Stanton-Anthony era were "all of them" victims "of some peculiar thwarting personal experience."[28])

Tarbell then launches into an extended defense of the homemaker against what she viewed as the corrosive influences of industrialism and feminism. In the Titusville of her nonage, the author notes, "the girl had her economic place" within a productive and bustling household. But at twentieth century's dawn the young woman, her place taken by machines and professionals, "is parasitical and demoraliz[ed]. . . . She concludes that if she is to serve she must seek something to do in some remote city. . . . The loss to communities of their educated young women, who find no response to their need, no place to serve in their own society, is incalculable." Factory girls, too, would be "healthier and happier at home"[29]: the trick was to liberate them from the yoke of industrial employment, and, to that end, Tarbell prescribed schooling to make women "scientific managers" of the household, for the nation's well-being depends on "the women who are at the great business of founding and filling those natural social centers which we call homes."[30]

Tarbell counted the cost of a woman's success in such a man's field as politics: "She must suppress her natural emotions. . . . She must overcome her own nature, put it in bonds, cripple it. . . . She *is* cold, also she is self-centered."[31] She must, perforce, neglect "the most essential obligation in a Woman's Business," which is "establishing her household on a sound moral basis."[32] Tarbell feared that this task was being placed on "other shoulders"—as, indeed, the prophetic feminist Charlotte Perkins Gilman had predicted when she wrote that "the home of the future is one in which not one stroke of work shall be done except by professional people who are paid by the hour."[33]

Unkind critics have charged Tarbell with self-loathing: she never married or had children; she was a famously successful career woman; who was she to lecture others on a "Woman's Business" that she herself had not practiced? Yet she remained, always, a Tarbell of Titusville, and she felt an overwhelming sororal affection for those women who had chosen a different path. Malicious "conservatives," too, revile Tarbell because she did not drop to her knees and worship the trusts and monopolies that had nearly destroyed her father and friends, but then her politics had a voluntaryist streak that confounds the dimwits.

Why, she asked, do women need the vote when they already have the power to right wrongs, if only they would try? She told a story—and was later ridiculed for it—that illumes her Titusville soul:

I can remember the day when the Beef Trust invaded a certain Middle Western town. The war on the old-time butchers of the village was open. . . . The women of the town had a prosperous club which might have resisted the tyranny which the members deplored, but the club was busy that winter with the study of Greek drama! They deplored the tyranny, but they bought the cut-rate meat—the old butchers fought to a finish, and the housekeepers are now paying higher prices for poorer meat and railing at the impotency of man in breaking up the Beef Trust![34]

Anna Howard Shaw, president of the NAWSA, made fun of Tarbell "for saying that women could have defeated the Beef Trust by patronizing independent butchers,"[35] and this cleavage is instructive: Tarbell, the small-*d* democrat, insisted that neighborly women acting in concert could slay giants, while the Methodist preacher Shaw put her faith in the votes of a mass of undifferentiated strangers petitioning the central state to erect a regulatory apparatus. So who's the radical and who's the reactionary?

THE SNOOP SISTERS

Ida Tarbell denied that "we can be saved morally, economically, socially by laws and systems"[36]: we must save ourselves, and we won't do it with a measly vote. "Outside the political machinery there is a world . . . where all reform begins," wrote a contributor to *The Anti-Suffragist* newspaper.[37] The Antis, for the most part, did *not* insist that a woman's place was in the home, at least not exclusively: it was also in the literary club, the association, the child welfare league, the hospital board—anywhere but the polling place and elective office. For "in a proper division of duty," asserted Alice Ranney Allen, "we have better work to do along civic, sanitary, and philanthropic lines."[38]

On this point the Antis were united, but beyond this everything falls apart, as the progressives, classical liberals, traditionalists, and anarchists who jostled within the ranks held vastly differing views on the role of the state in human affairs.

Many Antis took an acute interest in the goings-on in other homes. The reader of libertarian bent must stop every few paragraphs to scream, "Mind Your Own Business!" at the likes of Grace Duffield Goodwin, author of the the manifesto *Anti-Suffrage: Ten Good Reasons*. Mrs. Goodwin kicks things off with a fortifying epigraph from abolitionist (and suffragist) Wendell Phillips: "The agitator must stand outside of organizations, with no bread to earn, no candidate to elect, no party to save, no object but truth—to tear a question open and riddle it with light."

While Goodwin shunned the ballot, she urged women to poke their bluenoses into every dark corner in the land. She desired a national uniform divorce law; the censorship of motion pictures; and legislation interfering with the sale of alcohol, the labor of children, and the conduct in dance halls. "Bearing children and making homes" were, to Goodwin, "services rendered the state"[39]—an all too common locution. Josephine Dodge, president of the NAOWS and a founder of the day nursery movement in New York City, said of Woman: "the state must surround her with protective legislation in order that she may be most efficient where the state demands her highest efficiency."[40]

When bearing children and making homes are done for the greater glory of the state, look out.

The protective legislation Mrs. Dodge wanted took many forms. The Massachusetts Antis boasted of their state's Maternity Act, prohibitions of night work, and mothers' pensions, while noting the absence of such progressive nostrums in most of the western suffrage states. The implication was that woman suffrage, rooted in an ideology of individual rights, went hand in hand with the minimal night-watchman state. Limit the vote to males, on the other hand, and the paternalistic state would flower, as chivalrous legislators labored day and night to keep the ladies unsullied.

The two sides were forever engaged in a game of Pin the Brewer on the Enemy. In the lurid melodrama favored by suffragist publicists, the Antis served as "a cloak for the liquor elements."[41] (And the agents for bibulous German and Southern European immigrants.) The meddling crones of the Woman's Christian Temperance Union had endorsed suffrage in 1880, and the fear of some men was that a troop of righteous voting women would trample out the vintage where the grapes of wine are stored. (Recall that Senator James W. Wadsworth, Jr., of New York was defeated in 1926, largely as a result of his vocal opposition to both Prohibition and woman suffrage.)

But precious few Antis defended the right of their men to drain a bottle. They tut-tutted the public drunkenness so prevalent in the frontier suffrage states and hailed the progress of mandatory temperance in the vote-less East. The Reverend Theodore Cuyler, a New Yorker, turned the tables by warning that suffrage would unleash "an army of beer-drinking women [who] would swarm out of the slums and the tenement houses to reinforce the army of beer-drinking and whisky drinking men in favor of the dram shop."[42]

As usual, Mencken took a more jaundiced view, hitting the male on the head. He doubted that balloting women would drown the nation in milky purity: "Every normal woman believes, and quite accurately, that the average man is very much like her husband, John, and she knows very well that John is a weak, silly and knavish fellow, and that any effort to convert him into an archangel overnight is bound to come to grief."[43]

In any event, busybodies such as Mrs. Goodwin and the ladies of the WCTU were precisely the reason why Emma Goldman, the notorious "Red Emma," turned her formidable scorn upon woman suffrage. No treacly poet of the hearthstone—she called the home "this modern prison with golden bars"—Goldman also denounced the ballot as "an evil" that women should not be granted.[44]

The consequences for personal liberty would be disastrous if women got the vote. "Woman, essentially a purist, is naturally bigoted and relentless in her effort to make others as good as she thinks they ought to be," railed Goldman. "Thus, in Idaho . . . prostitution and gambling have been prohibited. In this regard the law must needs be of feminine gender: it always prohibits."[45]

"Instead of elevating woman," Goldman thundered, suffrage

> has made her a political spy, a contemptible pry into the private affairs of people, not so much for the good of the cause, but because, as a Colorado woman said, "They like to get into houses they have never been in, and find out all they can." . . . Woman's narrow and purist attitude toward life makes her a greater danger to liberty wherever she has political power.[46]

Red Emma's animadversions upon women found occasional echo among the more eccentric Antis. Edith Melvin, a Massachusetts businesswoman, sighed, "The instability of the female mind is beyond the comprehension of the majority of men. The charm, the 'sweet unreasonableness,' the lack of power of consecutive thought upon any intricate problem": these boded ill for a republic of bisexual balloting.[47]

Even more, shall we say, sweetly unreasonable, was Miss Annie Bock, former secretary of the California Political Equality League, whose apostasy won her a brief fame. "A year in politics has taught me that women are intolerant, radical, revolutionary and more corrupt in politics than men," she announced. (The Golden State had enacted woman suffrage in 1911.) "Woman is impulsive; she does not inform herself; she does not study; she does not consider the consequences of a vote. In her haste to remedy one wrong she opens the way to many. The ballot in her hands is a dangerous thing."[48]

Well, yes, agreed the Antis, but not in the way that the gynophobic Miss Bock meant. A covey of daft magpies was unlikely to fly to the polls and vote in a revolutionary regime. Indeed, in the first presidential election following the ratification of the Nineteenth Amendment, most women voted for Warren G. Harding, a peacemaker, budget-cutter, and relative civil libertarian. The horrors of the late teens—the frying of doughboys in the First World War, conscription, the jailing of pacifists and socialists, Prohibition—were done on man's watch.

The greater danger was espied by Father Walsh of Troy, who recoiled from the sight of women "amidst all the filth, obscenity, blasphemy and perjury of our modern polling-booth."[49] Close your eyes and the Anti condemnations of the sordidness of the whole exercise of voting sound a lot like those of Emma Goldman. Indeed, a strain of anarchism did run through the more provocative Anti writings. Across the sea, G. K. Chesterton bemoaned the suffrage movement as a surrender of women to men. The coercion that defines the state, wrote Chesterton, "should be conducted in the presence of some permanent protest on behalf of a humane anarchy," and that protest is the job of women. "Not only is one half of the good man an anarchist, but the anarchist is his better half; the anarchist is his wife." Declared Chesterton: "Woman would be more herself if she refused to touch coercion altogether."[50]

After all, Mrs. Lyman noted, "It is just where the law cannot reach that woman is supreme."[51]

And yet, the home was not really so impregnable. The progressives—including many Antis—had inspected the American home and found it wanting. Parents sent children to work in mills or hawk newspapers on grimy street corners: this must be stopped by child-labor laws. Some moms and dads were lax when it came to sending junior off to school every morning: this negligence must be overcome by compulsory education laws. Many men were roaring drunks, too besotted to be good fathers and munitions plant workers: their purchase of spirituous potables must be prohibited.

So many wrongs to right, and so little power. Wordy Jane Addams explained her support for suffrage with the contention that women had failed "to discharge their duties to their own household properly simply because they do not perceive that as society grows more complicated it is necessary that woman shall extend her sense of responsibility to many things outside of her own home if she would continue to preserve the home in its entirety."[52] Vigilant women, armed with the vote, could conscript an army of meat inspectors, school nurses, and juvenile judges. A few mossbacks and anarchists might still believe that the home was a castle inviolate, but the clear-eyed could see that the moat had been filled and the walls were disintegrating, Usher-like.

Mrs. Rudolph Blankenburg, a Pennsylvania suffragist, made this point well:

> We may shut our windows and bar the doors in our efforts to keep politics out of the home, but all such efforts are futile. Politics enter through the water pipes, through the gas mains, through the air we breathe, and the food we eat. It is quite time that the home-maker had a voice in saying what kind of politics shall invade her realm.[53]

And how could the Antis respond? By turning off politics at its source, as one would a leaky pipe. But far too many Antis had bought into the progressive assumptions about the benignant efficacy of the state. They consented to—even lobbied for—the interference of government agents in family relations, especially those of immigrant and Catholic families. Without the sturdy philosophical base of the traditionalists or the anarchists, they simply collapsed.

Lily Rice Foxcroft, a Massachusetts Anti, explained, "The strongest motive for anti-suffrage action is the deepening dread of woman suffrage as a menace to the home."[54] The home is no less menaced today, and while voting ladies are not the problem, Ida Tarbell, Ruth Whitney Lyman, and the Sisters left a trail, long-since overgrown, that just might lead us in a more humane direction.

Meanwhile, come every fourth November, my wife and I cheerfully vote for different presidential candidates, and then argue over which video to rent the following night.

NOTES

1. Quoted in Anne M. Benjamin, *A History of the Anti-Suffrage Movement in the United States from 1895 to 1920* (Lewiston, N.Y.: Edwin Mellen Press, 1991), pp. 277–78.

2. Jane Jerome Camhi, "Women against Women: American Anti-Suffragism, 1880–1920" (Ph.D. diss., Tufts University, 1973), p. 363.

3. Manuela Thurner's revisionist essay "Better Citizens without the Ballot" indicts "women's historians" who "all too often uncritically adopt feminist perspectives and judgments when they set out to write women into history." Thurner convincingly argues that the Antis—at least the articulate and visible Antis—were progressives who "tried to hold on to what they considered to be a distinctive female public realm, different from the male realm of politics." Thurner credits the Antis with "stimulat[ing] women to venture beyond the home dutifully to shoulder their responsibilities" in the realms of "reform and civic activities." Manuela Thurner, "Better Citizens without the Ballot," in *One Woman, One Vote*, ed. Marjorie Spruill Wheeler (Troutdale, Oreg.: NewSage Press, 1995), pp. 203–20. For a typically snide dismissal of the Antis, see Mara Mayor, "Fears and Fantasies of the Anti-Suffragists," *Connecticut Review* 7, no.2 (April 1974): 64–74.

4. Molly Elliot Seawell, *The Ladies' Battle* (New York: Macmillan, 1911), p. 113. An interesting subsidiary argument used by the Antis was that the state rests on brute force. Each vote is a token of compulsion, and "no electorate has ever existed, or ever can exist, which cannot execute its own laws," as Mrs. Seawell wrote. "To create an electorate unable to use physical force, is not, as the suffragists seem to think, merely doubling the present electorate. It means pulling out the underpinning, which is force, from every form of government the world has yet known." Seawell, pp. 27–28.

Mrs. Arthur M. Dodge concurred: "The vote of the man is a sort of contract to support the verdict of the ballot box, if need be, by the jury box, the cartridge belt, the sheriff's summons." Mrs. Arthur M. Dodge, "Woman Suffrage Opposed to Woman's Rights," *Annals of the American*

Academy of Political and Social Science 56 (November 1914): 99. To which the suffragists replied, why not disfranchise weak or invalided men?

5. Even most of the staunchest Antis conceded the injustice of "individuals who own property and pay taxes with no voice in public matters"; they often favored limited suffrage on school matters. Grace Duffield Goodwin, *Anti-Suffrage: Ten Good Reasons* (New York: Duffield and Company, 1913), p. 5.

6. The author's position is similar to that of Kate Gordon, leader of southern suffrage forces and organizer of the Louisiana Woman Suffrage Association, who joined the Antis to lobby southern legislatures to reject the Susan B. Anthony amendment on states-rights grounds. Miss Gordon was pro-woman suffrage but opposed to the federal amendment: a Tertium Quid, not really trusted by either side.

7. Seawell, p. 14.

8. Quoted in Mrs. Thomas Allen, "Woman Suffrage Versus Womanliness," *Anti-Suffrage Essays by Massachusetts Women* (Boston: Forum, 1916), p. 78.

9. Ida Tarbell, *The Business of Being a Woman* (New York: Macmillan, 1912), p. 211.

10. Francis Parkman, "Some of the Reasons Against Woman Suffrage," *Pamphlets Printed and Distributed by the Women's Anti-Suffrage Association of the Third Judicial District of the State of New York* (Littleton, Colo.: Fred B. Rothman & Co., 1990 [1905]), pp. 6–7.

11. Seawell, p. 12.

12. Alice N. George, "Suffrage Fallacies," *Anti-Suffrage Essays by Massachusetts Women*, pp. 25–29.

13. Ruth Whitney Lyman, "The Anti-Suffrage Ideal," *Anti-Suffrage Essays by Massachusetts Women*, p. 119.

14. Anne Hathaway Gulick, "The Imperative Demand upon Women in the Home," *Anti-Suffrage Essays by Massachusetts Women*, p. 128.

15. Lyman, pp. 119–20.

16. Elizabeth Jackson, "Suffrage and the School Teacher," *Anti-Suffrage Essays by Massachusetts Women*, pp. 85–87.

17. Quoted in Benjamin, p. 133.

18. Mrs. Francis M. Scott, *Pamphlets*, p. 1.

19. Quoted in Camhi, p. 18.

20. H. L. Mencken, *In Defense of Women* (New York: Time, 1950 [1922]), p. 111.

21. Annie Nathan Meyer, "Woman's Assumption of Sex Superiority," *North American Review* 178 (1904): 107–8.

22. Elizabeth McCracken, "The Women of America: Fourth Paper—Woman's Suffrage in Colorado," *The Outlook* 75 (1903): 743.

23. Quoted in Camhi, p. 324.

24. Minnie Bronson, former agent of the Federal Bureau of Labor and a progressive Anti, contended that a voting woman would forfeit her right to protective legislation and would have to compete with men, on the floor and in the pit, on equal terms: "Possessing the ballot, the woman who works must stand on an equality with men, and ask no favors; must accept the conditions imposed upon her by the law of supply and demand, and give as much toil as he, although no increase in physical vitality will respond to this demand." Quoted in Goodwin, pp. 60–61. Grace Duffield Goodwin mourned, "We conserve Niagara, and throw away young American girlhood." Goodwin, p. 90.

25. Quoted in Benjamin, p. 82.

26. "Woman Suffrage," *Popular Science Monthly*, in *Pamphlets*, p. 1. One literary lady who did speak out for the ballot was Mary Johnston, daughter of the Confederacy and organizer of the Equal Suffrage League of Virginia. She wrote *Hagar*, a prosuffrage novel, at the suggestion of Fola La Follette.

27. Tarbell, p. 26.

28. Quoted in Camhi, p. 291.

29. Tarbell, pp. 169–75.

30. Ibid., p. 242.

31. Ibid., pp. 42–43.

32. Ibid., p. 78.

33. Quoted in Lily Rice Foxcroft, "Suffrage a Step toward Feminism," *Anti-Suffrage Essays by Massachusetts Women*, p. 142.

34. Tarbell, pp. 65–66.

35. Kathleen Brady, *Ida Tarbell: Portrait of a Muckraker* (New York: Putnam, 1984), p. 202.

36. Quoted in Camhi, p. 311.

37. Quoted in Thurner, p. 211.

38. Alice Ranney Allen, "Woman Suffrage vs. Womanliness," *Anti-Suffrage Essays by Massachusetts Women*, p. 78.

39. Goodwin, p. 115.

40. Dodge, p. 101.

41. Quoted in Benjamin, p. 171.

42. Theodore L. Cuyler, "Shall Women be Burdened with the Ballot?" *Pamphlets*, p. 3.

43. Mencken, p. 110.

44. Emma Goldman, "Woman Suffrage," *Red Emma Speaks*, ed. Alix Kates Shulman (New York: Schocken Books, 1983), pp. 191–92.

45. Ibid., p. 196.

46. Ibid., p. 197.

47. Edith Melvin, "A Business Woman's View of Suffrage," *Anti-Suffrage Essays by Massachusetts Women*, p. 41.

48. Quoted in Benjamin, pp. 52, 71.

49. Father Walsh, "Protest against Woman Suffrage," *Pamphlets*, p. 1.

50. G. K. Chesterton, "The Modern Surrender of Women," in *As I Was Saying*, ed. Robert Knille (Grand Rapids, Mich.: Eerdmans, 1985), pp. 140–41.

51. Lyman, p. 126.

52. Jane Addams, "Why Women Should Vote," in *One Woman, One Vote*, p. 195.

53. Quoted in Benjamin, p. 150.

54. Foxcroft, p. 141.

4

I Shall Make America Over: The New Deal, Subsistence Homesteads, and the American Dream

> In nineteen thirty-five
> We began to arrive
> From empty mine and wasted timber-line
> And farms that no longer could thrive.
> Back to the plow and land
> By the sweat of our brow and our hand,
> To build from the start
> With faith in our heart
> As shoulder to shoulder we stand.
> —Ballad of the Tygart County (West Virginia) homesteaders[1]

In the midst of the Depression, when a thousand cranks and wise men were hollering ways to climb out from the slough, the fickle President Franklin D. Roosevelt took a fancy to an idea that had been promoted for the last decade by Americans as diverse as Henry Ford, director King Vidor (who personally financed the stirring propaganda film *Our Daily Bread*), and—critically—his wife, Eleanor. The idea was the subsistence homestead.

"Independence means self-dependence," preached Ford. "No unemployment insurance can be compared to an alliance between a man and a plot of land. With one foot in industry and another foot in the land, human society is firmly balanced against most economic uncertainties."[2]

The champions of subsistence homesteads were not back-to-the-land purists. They accepted the inevitability of the industrial economy and an increasingly mechanized agriculture; given a New Deal policy that paid farmers to destroy crops and slaughter livestock, the last thing they wanted was to breed new commercial farmers.

But the dream, as expressed by Mrs. Roosevelt, represented what we might call the Jeffersonian face of the New Deal:

Families engaged in subsistence farming consume their own garden products locally instead of sending them to distant markets. They are not expected to support themselves entirely by raising food, like the successful commercial farmers of the country. The plan is that they shall be situated near enough to an industry for one member of the family to be employed in a factory a sufficient number of days in the year to bring in the amount of money needed to pay for the things which the families must have and cannot produce. . . . Subsistence farms will make possible shorter hours of work in the factories as well as the decentralization of crowded populations.[3]

Well, that was the theory, anyway. Most of the New Deal's subsistence homesteads were crashing failures. Bureaucracy and poor planning were partly to blame, but so was human nature. It is not mutable—no matter how many directives Washington gives.

MILBURN AND REXFORD

Journalist Russell Lord recalled, "It is extraordinary what an emotional appeal a vision of a little white house with green shutters, forty acres, or four acres, and a mule, exerted . . . at the time of the 1933 bank holiday, and during the continuing spell of widespread unemployment afterward."[4]

It even bewitched the president, who was, after all, a rural man, albeit a Dutch patroon from the Hudson Valley (whose peasant neighbors were unimpressed: FDR ran for office nine times and won his hometown but thrice). In his major Topeka farm speech of September 14, 1932, candidate Roosevelt saw the pendulum "swinging back from the intense concentration of population in the cities." This "did not mean a 'back-to-the-land' movement in the ordinary sense of a return to agriculture" but rather "definite efforts to decentralize industry."[5] Or so said the professor who ghosted the speech, M. L. Wilson.

Milburn Lincoln Wilson—always M. L., and you can't blame him for that—was a folksy professor, a believer in "scientific agriculture," whose personal trinity consisted of the pastoral Irish poet George Russell, Abraham Lincoln, and John Dewey. Wilson had been born in 1885 to a prosperous farm family in Atlantic, Iowa, the town that, two generations later, would produce a rather more radical democrat, the historian William Appleman Williams.

The westward wind blew Wilson to Montana, where, after laboring as a wheat farmer and state extension agent, he became the star of the Montana State agricultural economics faculty. His complex plan for crop production controls attracted the attention of Rexford G. Tugwell, the Columbia economist who had insinuated himself into FDR's inner circle; Wilson met FDR, the two hit it off, and before you could say "networking" the Montana "mild man with wild ideas"[6] was on a train to Washington.

In 1927, Wilson laid out, in personal terms, the philosophy that underpinned his work:

All our inherited, romantic notions about the separateness of American farming and of the American farm home stand opposed to these great changes that are at our door. . . . We stand *now* . . . in the midst of a revolutionary mechanization of agriculture that will . . . remove from agriculture all but the ablest of those now engaged in it. It will wipe out the remaining differences, distances, and distinctions between country and city people. . . . I've been changing my mind . . . about the "independence" of the diversified, one-family farm. I know all the advantages. I had them myself when I was young. But I also know that the average farm-family income . . . is less than $1500 a year. . . . What kind of "independence" is that?

The place I'm most interested in, right now, is Utah, with its farming towns and villages. I was out there recently. I saw farmsteads along streets. The families who lived there weren't making, many of them, any more than $1500 a year. But because their houses were together and because a great deal of their work was shared or consolidated, those families had leisure. . . .

I got to wondering what would have come out of it, if my mother, laboring most of her life on our old homestead there in Cass County, Iowa, could have been a farmwife in a village like this. . . . She was a trained musician and an artist. But it kept her so busy taking care of all of us out there in the country, under isolated conditions, without conveniences, that she never had time to go ahead with her music or to paint. . . . When she was getting on toward seventy, I conceived the idea of getting her an easel and the materials for painting. You wouldn't believe the joy she got out of it! . . . She was a woman of genuine artistic ability, with a fine mind. Between the time that she was twenty and the time that she was seventy, that side of her never really had a chance to live at all. I don't believe that any amount of $1500 "independence" is worth that price.[7]

So Wilson resolved to recreate Utah's villages in Nebraska and California—leaving out the Mormonism, of course, which may also have been the mortar.

M. L. Wilson was a rumpled and well-liked man who accepted a planned economy as the wave of the future, though he insisted that it must be democratic, decentralized, and "brought about by 'the will of the people.' "[8] His ideal subsistence homestead would consist of twenty-five to one hundred families living in single-family homes on plots of one to five acres; each would have a vegetable garden, a pig, a cow, poultry, and share in a community orchard. A small industry would furnish the men with part-time wages. The extension service and nearby agricultural colleges would offer helpful advice; Washington would provide the seed money and then stand back and watch a newly self-sufficient settlement grow.

This was maudlin hogwash to Wilson's sponsor in the New Deal Brain Trust, Rexford Guy Tugwell. Has ever an American bureaucrat had a more aptly finicky and prissy name? Tugwell was a walking caricature, the embodiment of the supercilious don mocked by the great Milo Reno, fiery populist president of the Iowa Farmers Union: "You know of course about this latest 'Brain-trust' of half-baked college men. In the old days they became preachers, but now whenever a boy is entirely effeminated they send him to college and make him a professor. When he isn't any good at that they put him in the Cabinet as one of the Braintrusters."[9] (Even FDR's house farmers drew Reno's wrath: he loved to excoriate the secretary of agriculture as "Lord Corn Wallace.")

But back to Rexford Guy Tugwell: he was a debonair rich kid, the arrogant son of a canning factory owner on Lake Ontario's New York shore.[10] Often reviled as the ne plus ultra of snobbish urban liberals, his roots were rural, and late in life he wrote bloodless remembrances of Upstate, which had once been lovely but was now just "a backwater, and only the lethargic and ambitionless would stay to see its withering." (His recollections do not exactly drip with sentiment: of his late mother's poetry he wrote: "her output of what I am afraid was very bad verse was immense.")[11]

Tugwell is perhaps the least libertarian figure in American history. He broadcast his intentions in a poem he published while an undergraduate:

> I am strong
> I am big and well-made, I am muscled and lean and nervous,
> I am frank and sure and incisive.
>
> I bend the forces untamable;
> I harness the powers irresistible—
> All this I do; but I shall do more.
>
> I am sick of a nation's stenches,
> I am sick of propertied czars . . .
> I have dreamed my great dream of their passing,
> I have gathered my tools and my charts;
> My plans are fashioned and practical;
> I shall roll up my sleeves—make America over![12]

And this is pretty much what Rexford Tugwell—whom sycophants called "the Adonis of the Brain Trust"—tried to do: regiment society, plan everything, and deputize social scientists to oversee the vast prison that would be America. The New Deal can be thought of as a synthesis of Wilson and Tugwell, but in any such admixture the Tugwell component will always dominate. Just add cyanide to your next glass of water and take a swig.

THE INEFFABLE ELEANOR

The subsistence homesteads that Wilson and Tugwell were to run, then run into the ground, were authorized by the National Industrial Recovery Act of 1933. Senator John H. Bankhead (D-AL), Tallulah's uncle, slipped $25 million into the bill for the purpose of "aiding the redistribution of the overbalance of population in industrial centers." The legislative language was somewhat misleading; it conjured images of boxcars bursting with indigent Bowery bums being shipped to Kansas for the coming foison. Not that this wasn't a common reverie: publisher Bernarr Macfadden, who retained a lobbyist to spread the homestead word on Capitol Hill, wanted to "take people out of the bread line and put them upon land and give them some coarse food and implements that are essential to work the land and enable them to raise their own vegetables."[13]

But M. L. Wilson, who became the first director of the Division of Subsistence Homesteads, had a different plan. He saw his mission as the creation of "rural communities" in which "people can work part-time in factories at industrial pursuits, and derive an increased cash income from this employment while at the same time giving part of their time to self-sufficient agriculture." These "rurban" communities would "combine [the] blessings of industrial civilization with the social stability and the social health that are characteristic of a settled rural life."[14]

Unfortunately, the Division of Subsistence Homesteads was placed in the Department of the Interior, whose secretary, Harold Ickes, was a Chicago lawyer and irksome political hack who thought the whole idea of recreating self-sufficient rural communities was syrupy nonsense.

Hostility from farm organizations, which suspected the homesteads as potential competitors, kept the program out of the Agriculture Department, where it would have at least had a sympathetic chieftain in Henry Wallace. The Iowan—and why do all stories about rural politics lead back to Iowa?—was convinced that

The unemployment problem, combined with our paved roads and the ready transmission of electric power, together with the inherent love of humanity for open spaces, trees, animals, and all that kind of thing, make decentralization inevitable. . . . We are more than economic men. Somehow, I can't help thinking that the self-subsistence homesteads, if experimented with sufficiently by men of scientific, artistic and religious understanding, will eventually lead us a long way toward a new and finer world.[15]

Wilson and his comrades were carried away by the sense of possibility. Their dream, no matter that the eidolon never materialized, was deeply American. Senator Bankhead thought he had established "a new basis for American society," which was going to restore "that small yeoman class which has been the backbone of every great civilization."[16] Wilson, a self-described "scientific humanist and conditioned optimist,"[17] forswore utopianism. These homesteads were going to be closer to Main Street than Brook Farm:

> Now this isn't something for everybody. It isn't for well-to-do people and it isn't for poor working people who are willing to go on the way they are, just be a part of the great jazz-age procession. It isn't a relief proposition, to be applied at random. It's a middle-class movement for selected people, not the top, not the dregs. . . . Not all Americans really belong to this jazz-industrial age. We're not all white-lighters, never satisfied, just excited. There are a great many of us, of all degrees of wealth and education, in all walks of life, who feel that they are outcasts of the jazz-industrial age, and who are looking for something more secure and satisfying.[18]

Wilson directed the division's first loan, of $50,000, to a thirty-five-home project outside Dayton, Ohio, which was the brainchild of the anarchist preacher of self-sufficiency, Ralph Borsodi.

Borsodi envisioned a community in which settlers built their own homes and grew their own crops on three-acre plots; a pasture and wood-lot would be owned collectively. Most of the men would have part-time employment in Dayton, but the home would be the real "economic center of life." Borsodi enthused that the homesteads "are designed not only for family gardening but for family weaving and sewing and family activities in all the crafts which have been neglected for so many years." This was to be no mere Depression expedient: the loom-room and work-shop would "furnish [the] economic independence, security, and self-sufficiency" of "the early American home."[19]

It sounded nice. Alas, Borsodi was caught in a clash of management styles. Wilson's plan was for the Federal Subsistence Homesteads Corporation to make loans to local corporations, usually consisting of the leading citizens of a town, who would then be free to experiment with decentralized living in all its splendid multifariousness. But Ickes, his boss, was a devout centralist, who demanded that the locals take instructions from their betters in Washington. This was not, to put it mildly, Ralph Borsodi's "m.o.," and he quit, leaving Dayton Homesteads to come a cropper and providing yet another lesson to anarchists who ask for government loans.

The second Subsistence Homestead loan forever sullied the division's reputation.

M. L. Wilson's assistant administrator was Clarence E. Pickett, executive secretary of the American Friends Service Committee. Pickett and the Quakers had earlier undertaken various relief projects—food distribution, promoting gardening and canning clubs, the training of furniture makers and the development of the Mountaineer Craftsmen's Co-operative Association—in the coal country of West Virginia, Pennsylvania, Kentucky, and other states.

Much to the ultimate distress of homestead advocates, in 1933 Mrs. Roosevelt visited one particularly destitute area, near Morgantown, West Virginia. The First Lady traveled anonymously—she passed as a Philadelphia society matron—and the grinding poverty pained her. (She also became convinced "that with a little leadership there could develop in the mining areas, if not a people's revolution, at least a people's party patterned after some of the previous parties born of bad economic conditions."[20] Heaven forfend!)

What most affected the First Lady was a visit to one miner's shack:

As I went out [she later recalled], two of the children had gathered enough courage to stand by the door, the little boy holding a white rabbit in his arms. It was evident it was a most cherished pet. The little girl was thin and scrawny, and had a gleam in her eyes as she looked at her brother. Turning to me she said, 'He thinks we are not going to eat it, but we are,' and at that the small boy fled down the road clutching the rabbit closer than ever.[21]

Thereafter, the money flowed like water. The federal government purchased a 1,200 acre farm known as Arthurdale. FDR factotum Louis Howe impetuously ordered fifty prefabricated cottages to be shipped pronto, so that the jobless miners of Reedsville, West Virginia, could be domiciled in style by Thanksgiving 1933. The hasty Howe had ordered vacation homes, suited perhaps to a mild New England summer but not a harsh West Virginia winter. They were worthless to a Mountaineer family; all fifty had to be rebuilt.

Meanwhile, local agronomists recommended that the Arthurdale homes be set on high ground and that a community garden, to be farmed cooperatively, occupy the fertile lower land. This plan was rejected "because someone in Washington, who perhaps had never seen the tract," disliked it.[22]

Mrs. Roosevelt made Arthurdale her pet project. The cluster—one hesitates to call it a village—had "the look of a superior real-estate development."[23] Rhododendron were shipped 60 miles to add garniture."Planning," wrote a contemporary journalist, "was done for, rather than with, prospective homesteaders."[24]

Arthurdale's schools were placed under the scolding finger of a Vassar grad named Elsie Clapp, who declared "this is virgin soil"[25] and proceeded to operate a sprawling six-building school according to the principles laid down by her advisor, John Dewey. This was the only Subsistence Homestead school not run by the existing local school system, and it lasted but two years: the parents hated it, for, as Clarence Pickett lamented, Miss Clapp "assumed more experimental-mindedness among the homesteaders than had yet developed."[26]

"We have been spending money down there like drunken sailors,"[27] Harold Ickes complained of Arthurdale. He wrote in his diary:

> The President said that we could justify the cost, which will run in excess of $10,000 per family, by the fact that it is a model for other homestead projects. My reply to that was to ask what it was a model of, since obviously it wasn't a model of low-cost housing. . . . Wilson is not a good executive and under him Subsistence Homesteads got off to a very bad start. . . . Work down there has been extravagant and wasteful. . . . Mrs. Roosevelt, especially, has interfered all along the line, of course with the best intentions. As the President remarked to me, "My Missus, unlike most women, hasn't any sense about money at all."[28]

By July 1934, forty-three of the fifty reconstructed homes were occupied by the families of unemployed miners who had passed a battery of physical and mental examinations. Far from being down-and-outers, the Arthurdalians were "the very men likely first to get back on their own feet with a revival of business."[29] Each family received five acres, a cow, and a twenty-year mortgage.

Their gardens were in, but where were those who lacked the skill to make furniture for the craftsmen's co-op to work? A proposal that Arthurdale be given a contract to manufacture equipment for post offices was squashed in Congress by such old Jeffersonians as Representative Louis Ludlow (D-IN), who warned that subsidizing such a project "would lead the Government God knows where in the direction of sovietizing all industry. . . . [It] would sound the death knell of individual liberty in America."[30]

So most of the homesteaders were employed building homes for other prospective homesteaders in what threatened to be an endless chain. The Arthurdale Association, a co-op, later received loans to attract a vacuum-cleaner factory and a tractor plant, but these went belly-up. Then came the war; the mines reopened and the factories revved, producing war materiel. The experiment was over. The government quietly bowed out of the subsistence homesteads business.

What most rankled the good people of Arthurdale was the feeling that they were goldfish in a bowl. "Got so a man couldn't set down to his sow belly and turnip greens without some stranger peeking in at the window or walking in to ask fool questions," grumbled one settler.[31] The Arthurdalians were lab rats, not individuals. "It must be remembered," lectured one observer ready for the smock, "that the Federal Government and the states have established many experimental stations for the breeding of plants, trees, cattle, and horses"[32]—so why not people?

The project was factitious, not organic: "the homesteaders at Arthurdale are in Preston County but not of it," wrote one analyst. "Families cannot be set down in a ready-made community by social planners and be expected to adapt themselves efficiently to an environment in the development of which they have had little part."[33]

Mrs. Roosevelt later conceded that Arthurdale was "impractical." She'd had in mind the furniture factory she and her friend Nancy Cook had established some years earlier on the family's Hyde Park estate. The idea then had been to "furnish occupation for some of the younger men who would otherwise leave the farms."[34]

A not ignoble aim. But most of the New Deal projects were marred by a Great White Father paternalism—intellectuals designing houses and jobs for miners whose wives were bombarded, as Representative Guy Moser (D-PA) cracked, by "gratuitous advice by childless women who never kept house themselves."[35]

There were to be more Daytons and more Arthurdales. A total of thirty-four subsistence homestead communities were created. They were of three types: part-time farmers near existing industrial employment (as in Dayton); all-rural colonies for resettled submarginal farmers; and, à la Arthurdale, villages for "stranded workers," which would try to attract decentralized industry.

The problem with creating a community from scratch is that the whole thing is, literally, unreal. Matters that ought to be decided by voluntary human action over time are thrashed out in debates among intellectuals. For instance, should homesteaders endure privation, or must they be relatively cosseted? Roy Hendrickson, a Wilson staffer, recalled the arguments:

First, there was the [Bernarr] Macfadden or $150 a year school of thought. You know—fresh air is healthy. The soil is kind. There's lots of land out of the pulsing city, and about $150 a year is all you need. Live in a shack—not too many clothes—clothes are unnatural. And stick to vegetables, roots, herbs; only cave men crave meat. No concern for modern medical facilities; no vaccination. Back to nature!

Next step up were the $500 a year boys. Go out to cut-over land, rear cabins; from the extra logs rear a school. Make your own furniture; dig in; and twenty years from now maybe you can get all the settlers together and have a hospital raising.

. . . The next big school of thought on the question was the $1200 a year bunch. Here the shacks were to be on stubs or some foundation above the ground, cheap, no paint, until paint could somehow be earned, if ever; community baths and waterclosets, if any; and as for electricity or not, let that depend on where the place was—what electricity cost.

Most of us in the first Subsistence Homestead Office wavered somewhere between that and a $1500 minimum, allowing for adjustments upward and downward according to the natural prospects of the people and the place.

We were all with Wilson against strict standardization; we favored local architects and local planning. But in many places we found no local architects who could take on layouts and planning of whole colonies, so we came around to absentee urban architecture and planning, in places.[36]

(Thanks to Mrs. Roosevelt's pressure, homesteads generally had four to six rooms, baths, and electricity.)

Each project began with high hopes: the "rurban pattern of life . . . based upon a combination of industrial employment and agricultural activities"[37] that M. L. Wilson envisioned was finally to be realized! But then the dreams died, tangled up in rules. Wilson never found his Mormon villages but he did help place 120 Jewish needle-workers and their families on 1,200 acres outside Highstown, New Jersey. They paid $500 each for the privilege: the plan called for a co-op garment factory, truck garden, dairy, and poultry plant.

"Jersey Homesteads," wrote Paul Conkin, author of the standard study *Tomorrow a New World*, "as much as any other New Deal community, was a well-defined social organism, with a character and a soul all its own."[38]

Yet it failed. Its atrocious theme song didn't help:

> Production, co-operation,
> Freedom for every nation,
> Here, there and everywhere,
> This is our claim:
> Workers' Aim, Workers' Aim.[39]

The opposition of David Dubinsky, head of the International Ladies Garment Workers Union, delayed construction from 1933 until 1936–37; despite an experienced and dedicated workforce, the co-op lost enough money to make Eleanor Roosevelt blush. And the farm was a disaster: urban needle-workers were none too eager to slip on overalls and speed the plow, so Negro transients had to be shipped in to work the soil. Workers' aim, workers' aim.

By this time M. L. Wilson and his dogged hopefulness were long gone. In May 1934, Harold Ickes repudiated the local control concept and transferred all decision making to D.C.; one month later, a weary Wilson quit. In May 1935 the division, which had spent just a third of its original $25 million appropriation, was absorbed into the new Resettlement Administration, whose chief, alas for the doughty homesteaders, was Rexford Tugwell.

Tyrannosauras Rex looked askance at these silly exercises in agrarian nostaglia. He viewed Wilson and Henry Wallace as part of "a formidable conspiracy, one I had never been willing to join, to preserve the family farm at any cost. . . . I saw no reason why farming should be exempt from the general evolution of productive processes." The iron laws of economics dictated an agriculture which must be large-scale, mechanized, and subordinated to national interests: this "blind defense of the family farm" must be overcome.[40]

Tugwell later scoffed that FDR's "notion that industry could be returned in small units to rural sites with benefit both to industry and the country" simply "made no sense."[41] So he placed the subsistence homesteads on the back burner, where they would simmer for a few years more, as his Resettlement Administration "emphasized resettlement, technological development, and urbanization."[42] He had long despised "unguided land settlement," so the RA undertook the twin policies of reclamation and deracination: it sought to drive submarginal farmers into either efficient large cooperative farms or the cities, where enriching factory work awaited. The smart fellow would try "moving to a place where opportunity exists,"[43] as Tugwell had when he abandoned the shores of Lake Ontario for the chores of the Potomac.

Tugwell scorned the subsistence homesteads, for "no higher life can be built without an industrial basis."[44] His real passion within the RA was for the three "Greenbelt" cities (near Washington, Cincinnati, and Milwaukee), which were to be suburban refuges from the anarchy and *unplannedness* of the city and the superstitions of the country. "My idea," wrote Tugwell in 1935, "is to go just outside centers of population, pick up cheap land, build a whole community and entice people into it. Then go back into the cities and tear down whole slums and make parks of them."[45]

These three satellite cities, girdled by woodlands, were each to house populations of ten thousand: homes would be leased, not owned, and employment was to be found in the nearby cities. There were stores at Greenbelt, Maryland—a gas station, a barbershop, a drugstore, a movie theater—but only one of each: the devil Competition was proscribed. Clothes could not hang on lines after four P.M. No dogs were allowed. The city manager system was in effect: no disorderly democracy here. This was Rex Tugwell's utopia—he even lived in Greenbelt (briefly) in the 1950s—but for most it was a verdant hell. "Tenants often disliked the stiff discipline and desired to own their own homes as soon as possible," wrote Paul Conkin.[46] Again, human nature was not malleable.

By 1935 many Americans were sick of Rexford Tugwell, lean musculature or not. Hugh Johnson, the former administrator of the National Recovery Administration, joked: "Rex Tugwell knows as much about agriculture as Haile Selassie knows about Oshkosh, Wisconsin."[47] The vituperation spilled onto the RA, so Tug had to go: he quit after the 1936 election. In 1937 the RA was folded into the Farm Security Administration; the subsistence homesteads, by now the red-headed stepchildren of the New Deal, sputtered on for a few years more and were largely liquidated by 1948.

IS THAT ALL THERE IS?

So was it all a waste of time and money? Did Harold Ickes and Rexford Tugwell, the smug statists, know something that better people—M.L. Wilson and Eleanor Roosevelt—did not?

Not exactly. Yes, there were errors of rashness and organization. There were dismal failures, even disasters. One of the most egregious occurred in the development of the Cahaba community near Birmingham, Alabama. The Subsistence Homesteads Division had purchased land on which forty Negro families lived; the RA forced them out, burned their homes, and moved them to worthless land, while "white tenants moved into the beautiful new homes constructed on their old homesites." As one of the displaced recalled, "women folks knowed hardly what to do and we just went to cryen and cryen."[48]

The paternalism of social scientists who wanted to be gods was also a bane. In every settlement they placed a "community building," which in theory was to serve as a village green, a district school, and a dance hall rolled into one. Yet these edifices

indicated the social planners' desire to influence not only the economic and educational life of its community clients, but their social life as well. . . . The community buildings were criticized because they seemed to be attempts to isolate and separate the communities from the area in which they were located or because they indicated an attempt to tell people how to organize their social life when no expert had the right to do this. In many communities the community building was either not wanted or seldom used.[49]

Arthurdale and the three other colonies for "stranded workers" never figured out a way to attract private industry. The handful of rural co-ops set up by the Subsistence Homesteads Division fared badly because they were too far out of the American grain. The project managers retained tight control: the government "was afraid to turn the co-operative associations over to the inexperienced people of a community."[50] Farmers, imbued with the individualist American ethos that drove Rex Tugwell crazy, hankered for a chance to own their own land. As one Arkansawyer who headed a co-op told a Tugwell aide, "I believe a man could stick around here for five or six years and save enough money to go off and buy himself a little hill farm of his own."[51]

Rex Tugwell never could understand that impulse. He laid the failure of the collective farm project in Casa Grande, Arizona, squarely at the feet of the "poverty-stricken folk in the Southwest" he wanted to help. Casa Grande "came to grief not because the conception was bad or because the technique was mistaken but because the people there could not rise to the challenge. It was character which failed. . . . because the environment was hostile to the development of character."[52]

The environment, of course, was America; the character was Jeffersonian. And if Tugwell hated it all, M. L. Wilson did not. Wilson railed against "the crass materialism and the shallowness of the Jazz Age" not because he thought these frivolities distracted from the creation of the new Soviet Man but because he remembered, from Iowa and Montana, that there were other Americas, better Americas. "This is no way for people to live," he said of the congested East. "I want to get them out on the ground with clean sunshine and air around them, and a garden for them to dig in. . . . Spread out the cities, space the factories out, give people a chance to live."[53] And one or two homesteads did just that.

The successful homesteads took human nature and the American spirit into account. Americans want to own land, not lease it from governments or corporations. They want to order their own affairs, within families and in small self-governing communities. They do not despise outsiders, and they are willing to take advice if tendered in a spirit of fellowship, but they will not re-enact the old slave-massah game with anyone, no matter how many degrees he possesses.

Perhaps the most successful New Deal community, according to Paul Conkin and others, was Granger Homesteads in Iowa, which was also the only one in which "the agrarian, distributist school of thought remain[ed] important."[54]

Father Luigi G. Ligutti, pastor of the Catholic church in Granger, Iowa, a mining town, had been appalled by the "dirt and grime, impassable streets and unsanitary, unhealthy living conditions" of Granger's mining camps. The workers, wrote Ligutti, were either "completely at the mercy of the industrialists" or were mendicants on government relief.[55]

Father Ligutti formed a local corporation to apply for a Subsistence Homesteads grant; alack, the good priest's timing was off, for the loan was approved just as M. L. Wilson was being run off and Harold Ickes was centralizing control of all projects in Washington. Nevertheless, Father Ligutti pressed on: he secured a loan of $125,000, which purchased 224 acres on which to locate fifty (mostly mining) families. They were a polyglot lot, primarily Italian and Croatian Catholics, selected for their "industry, sobriety, honesty, responsibility, and thrift."[56] By December 1935 they had moved into four-to six-room homes—which were to be owned, not leased—on fertile five-acre plots of land. Each plot included either a barn or a combination garage-poultry house. The homes had electricity, modern plumbing, even phone service, if desired. Father Ligutti understood the reservations people had about the homestead program: they were reluctant to trade "a remotely possible, good future, in a commercial, postdepression life"[57] for the dread, the isolation, the back-breaking monotony that they imagined had marked farm life of years gone by.

The men would remain seasonally employed in the mines, but the gardens would prove bountiful. The women took quickly to canning, and, with the aid of the agricultural college at Ames, the Grangers prospered. "The large families, the good soil, the inherent love of the land present in many of the Europeans"[58] combined with the indefatigable Father Ligutti to make Granger the model subsistence homestead community. The padre said Mass on Sunday, taught in the parochial school on weekdays, and spent the rest of his time visiting the households, offering counsel, exhortation, and prayer. Most of the residents were Catholic—Granger was unique among homesteads in this respect—and the cohesion of a shared faith made this kin to M. L. Wilson's idealized Mormon villages. Children were to be more than mouths to feed: they worked the gardens, too, and as Father Ligutti noted, "They are out on the land, where . . . children are assets to the families, not liabilities."[59]

"Co-operative organization at Granger was less ambitious, but more successful,"[60] than at other homesteads, judged Paul Conkin. A credit union and cannery flourished; at school, children were taught the skills necessary for "Home Life on the Land." Unlike the organizers of Highstown, the needle-workers settlement, or Arthurdale—collectivists and paternalists—Father Ligutti professed the "familiar and well-tested axiom that a government governs best which governs least."[61] He deplored the interference of Ickes and Tugwell, but Granger remained, under his guidance, at once individualistic and cooperative.

Father Ligutti saw the homestead movement as necessary if "there is to be any material or spiritual salvation for our America. . . . Direction of the people to the land; keeping the people on the land; encouraging the people to hold to the land, to work with the land, to love the land is practical as well as poetical. There is both poetry and sound economics in such a community as Granger."[62]

THE GHOST OF TOM JOAD

M. L. Wilson liked to tell of going home to visit the family farmstead in Cass County, Iowa. He called upon an old neighbor and sat on the porch drinking buttermilk and arguing about the New Deal until sundown. "When I left," Wilson recalled, "he walked as far as the gate with me and put his hand on my shoulder: 'Milburn, I want you to promise me something. I want you to go out and stand for a little while in the old churchyard where your grandfather is buried.'"

Wilson was moved. But then the codger added, "And Milburn, when you're out there I want you to notice how the sod's all tore up from that old fellow whirling over and over in his grave!"[63]

Much of the New Deal, with its emphasis on a planned economy and regimented society, was an affront to American traditions. But the subsistence homesteads program was not.

Clarence E. Pickett remained proud of his efforts at Arthurdale:

We had a strong feeling that while we had built the facade of abundant production in this country higher and higher . . . we had forgotten that the hearth where the family gathers and where neighbors are welcomed is at the very heart of human life. We were trying again to put the welfare of the home and the individuals who live in it in the center of our national interest.[64]

That dream is not a lie, and for many Americans, even those who despise the New Deal, it can never really die. The ghosts flicker on.

NOTES

1. Quoted in Russell Lord, *The Wallaces of Iowa* (Boston: Houghton Mifflin, 1947), p. 425.

2. "Mayors, Misery & Money," *Time*, June 13, 1932, pp. 13–14.

3. Eleanor Roosevelt, "Subsistence Farmsteads," *Forum* 91 (April 1934): 199.

4. Lord, p. 340.

5. Quoted in Richard S. Kirkendall, *Social Scientists and Farm Politics in the Age of Roosevelt* (Columbia: University of Missouri, 1966), p. 47.

6. Lord, p. 316.

7. Ibid., p. 304.

8. Quoted in Kirkendall, p. 20.

9. Quoted in John A. Crampton, *The National Farmers Union: Ideology of a Pressure Group* (Lincoln: University of Nebraska, 1965), p. 141.

10. The Sinclairville *Star* described Tugwell's father, Charles H. Tugwell, as "a popular, energetic, wide-awake young business man"—a Sinclair Lewis pop. Rexford G. Tugwell, *The Light of Other Days* (Garden City, N.Y.: Doubleday, 1962), p. 22.

11. Ibid., p. 26. This is truly a tedious memoir—even for as indiscriminate a reader as the author, whose taste for Upstate literature is such that he'd gladly read the Sinclairville phone book.

12. Quoted in Bernard Sternsher, *Rexford Tugwell and the New Deal* (New Brunswick, N.J.: Rutgers University Press, 1964), p. 5.

13. Quoted in Paul K. Conkin, *Tomorrow a New World* (Ithaca, N.Y.: Cornell University Press, 1959), p. 31.

14. O. E. Baker, Ralph Borsodi, and M. L. Wilson, *Agriculture in Modern Life* (New York: Harper & Brothers, 1939), p. 259.

15. Quoted in Lord, p. 413. In 1934 Secretary Wallace brought the Irish poet George Russell to Washington to give pep talks to the troops. The trip was sponsored by Mrs. Mary Harriman Rumsey—yes, of *that* Harriman family, so its revolutionary potential was limited. The eccentric Russell was hardly a new-dealer—he urged Wallace to look to the Transcendentalist poets, not the state, for guidance—but he wrote to Wilson: "I think you have the root of real humanity in you and what you do must be good." *Letters from AE*, ed. Alan Denson (London: Abelard Schuman, 1961), p. 218.

16. Quoted in Arthur M. Schlesinger, Jr., *The Coming of the New Deal* (Boston: Houghton Mifflin, 1958), p. 363.

17. Quoted in Lord, p. 295.

18. Ibid., pp. 420–21.

19. Ralph Borsodi, "Dayton, Ohio, Makes Social History," *The Nation*, April 19, 1933, p. 448.

20. Eleanor Roosevelt, *This I Remember* (New York: Harper & Brothers, 1949), p. 126. The homestead program as defuser of revolution was a common theme. William E. Brooks warned that West Virginia was filled with "ready fuel for the social incendiary's torch." After all, "stuck away behind the hills, crowded closely together, with no resources outside themselves and little there, people inevitably begin to think alike and can easily become the prey of trouble makers or demagogues." William E. Brooks, "Arthurdale—A New Chance," *Atlantic Monthly*, February 1935, p. 199. Bernard M. Baruch and Mrs. Henry

Morgenthau took a particular interest in Arthurdale: not auspicious patrons for a radical community.

21. Eleanor Roosevelt, p. 127.

22. Millard Milburn Rice, "Footnote on Arthurdale," *Harpers*, March 1940, p. 414.

23. Wesley Stout, "The New Homesteaders," *Saturday Evening Post*, August 4, 1934, p. 7.

24. Rice, p. 415.

25. Quoted in Conkin, p. 248.

26. Clarence E. Pickett, *For More than Bread* (Boston: Little, Brown, 1953), p. 59.

27. Quoted in Schlesinger, p. 366.

28. Harold L. Ickes, *The Secret Diary of Harold L. Ickes* (New York: Simon and Schuster, 1953), pp. 152, 218.

29. Stout, p. 62.

30. Quoted in Schlesinger, p. 367.

31. Quoted in Conkin, p. 255.

32. Brooks, p. 203.

33. Rice, p. 419.

34. Eleanor Roosevelt, p. 33.

35. Quoted in Conkin, p. 223.

36. Quoted in Lord, p. 427.

37. Quoted in Kirkendall, p. 74.

38. Conkin, p. 273.

39. Ibid., p. 268.

40. Rexford G. Tugwell, *The Brains Trust* (New York: Viking, 1968), p. 207. Yet Tugwell never bad-mouthed Wilson. The Iowan, Tugwell was to recall, "had the affection and trust of an extraordinary assortment of people. This wide acceptance was unusual in caustic intellectual circles." Tugwell, *The Brains Trust*, p. 206.

41. Quoted in Sternsher, p. 267. One of the funniest lines Arthur Schlesinger, Jr., ever penned was: "Of Tugwell's bonds with Roosevelt, the most intimate was their shared passion for the earth." Schlesinger, p. 361.

42. Kirkendall, pp. 112–13.

43. Ibid., p. 112.

44. Ibid., p. 43.

45. Quoted in Schlesinger, pp. 370–71. Tugwell had hoped to build twenty-five Greenbelt communities at first; thousands more would follow as he bent the nation to his will.

46. Conkin, pp. 319–20.

47. Quoted in Sternsher, p. 281. Al Smith said in 1936 that Tugwell should "get one of these racoon coats that college boys wear at a football

game and . . . go to Russia, sit on a cake of ice and plan all he wants."
Quoted in Kirkendall, p. 120.

48. Conkin, p. 202.

49. Ibid., p. 193.

50. Ibid., p. 209.

51. Quoted in Schlesinger, p. 372. Mrs. Roosevelt heard the same thing at her Hyde Park factory. She wrote:

> We found in our shop that as soon as a young man learned a trade in which he could make more money than he could on a farm he did not care enough about farm life to want to give up for the summer the good wages and regular hours he enjoyed in his trade . . . the young men sought the easier life with larger financial return. In this they were usually urged on by their wives, who felt that life on the farm was hard for them as well as for their husbands.

Eleanor Roosevelt, p. 34.

52. Rexford G. Tugwell, foreword to Edward C. Banfield, *Government Project* (New York: Free Press, 1951), pp. 11–12. Banfield's book is a detailed study of the Casa Grande collective. An ex-Farm Security Administration employee, Banfield concludes that the collective farm failed because the settlers "were engaged in a ceaseless struggle for power." Banfield, p. 231.

53. Quoted in Schlesinger, p. 363.

54. Conkin, p. 294.

55. Rt. Rev. Msgr. Luigi G. Ligutti and Rev. John C. Rawe, *Rural Roads to Security* (Milwaukee: Bruce, 1940), p. 171.

56. Ibid., p. 172.

57. Ibid., p. 182.

58. Conkin, p. 300.

59. Ligutti and Rawe, p. 181.

60. Conkin, p. 301.

61. Ligutti and Rawe, p. 173.

62. Ibid., pp. 184–85.

63. Quoted in Lord, p. 377. Wilson was forced out of the Department of Agriculture in 1953 by new secretary Ezra Taft Benson—didn't he know that the old New Dealer worshipped at the shrine of the Mormon village? Oddly, Wilson, the agrarian, was buried in Rock Creek Cemetery in Washington, while Tugwell was interred in the family plot in Sinclairville, New York. Who can ever know what is inside a man?

64. Pickett, p. 62.

5

Doesn't Anybody Stay in One Place Anymore? Good Roads, Interstate Highways, and the Asphalt Bungle

"Improvement makes strait roads; but the crooked roads without Improvement are roads of Genius."

—William Blake[1]

In 1956, as the highwaymen performed their equivalent of the Brinks Job—the creation of the National System of Interstate and Defense Highways—the prince of suctorial journalism, Theodore White, exulted in *Collier's*: "Men will be able to drive from New York to San Francisco scarcely, if ever, slowing at a traffic light."[2]

To which too few replied: Why should we want to do that?

. . . OR WHATEVER COMES OUR WAY

What is a road but the engineer-imagined path of least resistance? Hillaire Belloc, in a passage with enough passive constructions to make Strunk turn White, wrote: "It is the Road which determines the sites of many cities and the growth and nourishment of all. It is the Road which controls the developments of strategics and fixes the sites of battles. It is the Road that gives its frame-work to all economic development. It is the Road which is the channel of all trade and, what is more important, of all ideas."[3]

Just as trade and ideas were predominantly local prior to the growth of the modern state, so, too, was the building of roads. President Monroe's veto of the Cumberland Road bill in 1822 virtually ended any U.S. government role in the matter until 1916. The states, hip deep in the financing of rails and canals, had no time for mere foot and carriage paths.

In his standard history, *American Highway Policy* (1941), Charles L. Dearing wrote, "As late as 1880, exclusive responsibility for the provision of rural roads rested with local governments. Townships and road districts served as administrative units; management was amateur rather than professional; and a medieval system of 'working out the road tax' supplied the chief means of road support."[4]

This "extremely localized" system lacked uniformity: as township abutted township, a well-kept road might feed into a rutted one, and the smoothened and perfectly straight lines (gifts of eminent domain) that we cruise today were rare; more often, the traveler wove a zigzag route along the borders of farmers' lands.

Once or twice a year, men paid their road tax with a day's labor. To historian Dearing's disapproval, this day "came to be viewed more as the occasion for neighborhood social gatherings and the exchange of the latest accumulation of stories than as a tax contribution."[5] (The same had once been said of the militia.) Yet most townships took pride in their maintenance of roads; one of the towering American statesmen of the mid-nineteenth century, New York governor and 1868 Democratic presidential candidate Horatio Seymour, ended his political career supervising the repair of public roads as path-master of the town of Deerfield.

Then came preachers of the gospel of Improvement. At first they were bicyclists and bike manufacturers, agitating through the League of American Wheelmen. After all, it was no fun to be thrown head over handlebars just because some prideless rubes had roads more pockmarked than the moon. The coming of rural free delivery in 1897 spurred Uncle Sam's participation: neither rain nor sleet nor snow can stop the mail, but an impassable road can. The railroaders soon chimed in—to their eventual regret—eager to transport the people and provender that feeder roads could spill into town. The final, and soon to be dominant, fragment of the coalition was the fledgling automobile industry: not only carmakers but petroleum refiners, parts suppliers, motorists, and the newly confident—no, *empowered*—engineers and state highway officials.

Soon, a "good roads" movement was born, heralded by conventions and magazines, and who on earth could oppose good roads? New Jersey was the first (in 1891) to enact a state aid law; by 1917 every state had followed suit. The Federal Road Act of 1916 gifted the states with matching funds ($75 million over five years); it also required the creation of state highway departments, thus signing the death warrant for the town-county system of highway maintenance. "Working off the road tax" traveled lethewards aboard a horse and buggy; the labor tax gave way to disbursements from general funds or a tax on gasoline and parts. Professionals—with college degrees!—supplanted the amateurs. Rough-hewn freemen and civic leaders such as Horatio Seymour were replaced by men with capital letters and periods after their names. Decentralism had failed: as a good roads promoter named Chauncey—and what good has ever come of such a forename?—complained: "Neither of the Napoleons, nor both, could have ever made the roads of France the best in the world with 100 independent road overseers in each division of 100 square miles."[6]

Despite its matrix in the world of fancy-pants bicyclists and the automobile industry, the good roads movement tinctured its propaganda with populism. (Opposition to the 1916 law came from constitutionalists, the parsimonious, and New Englanders, who correctly viewed the legislation as a sectional subsidy of the South.)

Senator John Bankhead (D-AL), father of the prime mover of rural resettlement during the New Deal, made the agrarian case for good roads in 1908:

> Do not let us have great mobs of the unemployed, combining the scum of Europe with the misled boys from our American farms, so long as there are millions of acres of land waiting to be tilled and homes waiting to be built. Good roads will make farm life attractive; they will bring the isolated dweller closer to his neighbor, and I feel confident they will check the movement of our rural population to the great cities.[7]

The National Grange endorsed this position, adding the futile demand that road construction "be kept within the smallest possible unit of population . . . in order that the money appropriated . . . be spent close to the people most directly concerned."[8] Yet rural folks, despite the effusions of their representatives, by and large refused to join the good roads party. They "continually opposed any form of indebtedness to pay for road construction and insisted the government appropriations for road building be kept to a minimum and at the local level."[9]

One mandarin of the macadam, General Roy Stone, director of the federal Office of Road Inquiry, deplored the "negative or hostile attitude of the rural population towards all effective legislation in this direction."[10] Didn't the rustics know that better roads meant easier access to markets, bulging wallets, skyrocketing land values, healthier animals, and consolidated schools that would uplift their stupid striplings? The blessings of good roads were even reckoned in dollars: the Department of Agriculture estimated that bad roads had cost American farmers $600,000 in 1906.[11]

"Farmers never offered any alternative spending proposals,"[12] laments one historian of the South, but that's just the point: the real alternative was a status quo that many rather liked. For as with "national defense" and "education," "good roads" was a seemingly noncontroversial cause that carried within it the seeds of American reconstruction.

The mossback farmers, the men content to be mired in mud—that is, grounded at home—filled the columns of local newspapers with complaints about the taxes that good roads would bring, but it was left to literary men (who have consistently been the keenest dissenters from consensus politics) to make the perverse case for—bad roads. (Never underestimate the value of sloganeering. What decent fellow can oppose good roads and peacekeepers, or support assault weapons and fugitive warlords?) In *The Man Who Knew Coolidge* (1928), Sinclair Lewis of Sauk Centre, Minnesota, had his booster fire:

> When I first drove that road, it was just a plain dirt road running through a lot of unkempt farms, and now every mile or so you'd find a dandy up-to-date hot-dog stand . . . stocking every known refreshment for the inner man—hot dogs and apple pie and chewing-gum and cigars and so on and so forth—and of course up-to-date billboards all along the road to diversify it, and garages maybe every five miles, and in every town a dandy free auto camp providing free water and wood for the tourists. And so many of the farmers quitting their old toilsome routine and selling apples and cider to the motorists—I asked one of 'em, by the way, how he could keep his supply up, and come to find out, he didn't have an apple tree on the place—he got 'em all from a grocery store in the next town. Oh, motoring certainly has made a great and wonderful change in the country![13]

In 1930, the Tennessee novelist-essayist Andrew Lytle, in his contribution to the epochal agrarian volume *I'll Take My Stand*, took on the good roads movement. I shall quote Lytle at length, for his is that rare attack that was launched from love rather than niggardliness:

> The good-road programs drive like a flying wedge and split the heart of [southern] provincialism—which prefers religion to science, handcrafts to technology, the inertia of the fields to the acceleration of industry, and leisure to nervous prostration. Like most demagoguery, it has been advertised as a great benefit to the farmer. Let us see just what the roads have done and who they benefit? They certainly can be of no use to the farmer who cannot afford to buy a truck. He finds them a decided drawback. The heavy automobile traffic makes it hazardous for him even to appear on the main highways. But if he has the temerity to try them, they prove most unsatisfactory. Besides being a shock to his mules' feet, it is difficult for the team to stand up on the road's hard, slick surface.
>
> The large farmers and planting corporations who can afford to buy trucks are able to carry their produce to market with less wear

and tear than if they drove over rougher dirt pikes. But this is a dubious benefit, for the question is not between trucks on good or bad roads, but between teams on passable roads and trucks on arterial highways.

But in any case the farmer receives few direct profits. Asphalt companies, motor-car companies, oil and cement companies, engineers, contractors, bus lines, truck lines, and politicians—not the farmer—receive the great benefits and the profits from good roads. But the farmer pays the bills. The states and counties float bonds and attend to the upkeep on the highways and byways, and when these states are predominantly agricultural, it is the people living on the land who mortgage their labor and the security of their property so that these super-corporations may increase incomes which are now so large that they must organize foundations to give them away.

But the great drain comes after the roads are built. Automobile salesmen, radio salesmen, and every other kind of salesman descends to take away the farmer's money. The railroad had no such universal sweep into a family's privacy. It was confined to a certain track and was constrained by its organization within boundaries which were rigid enough to become absorbed, rather than absorb. But good roads brought the motor-car and made of every individual an engineer or conductor, requiring a constant, and in some instances a daily, need for cash. The psychological pressure of such things, and mounting taxes, induce the farmer to forsake the old ways and buy a ledger.

The great drain continues. The first thing he does is to trade his mules for a tractor. He has had to add a cash payment to boot, but that seems reasonable. He forgets, however, that a piece of machinery, like his mules, must wear out and be replaced; but the tractor cannot reproduce itself. He must lay aside a large sum of money against the day of replacement, whereas formerly he had only to send his brood mare to some jack for service.

The next thing it does, it throws his boys out of a job, with the possible exception of one who will remain and run it. This begins the home-breaking. Time is money now, not property, and the boys can't hang about the place draining it of its substance, even if they are willing to. They must go out somewhere and get a job. If they are lucky, some filling station will let them sell gas, or some garage teach them a mechanic's job. But the time is coming when these places will have a surfeit of farmer boys.

He next buys a truck. The gals wanted a car, but he was obdurate on that point, so he lost them. They went to town to visit kin, then gradually drifted there to marry or get a job. The time comes when

the old woman succumbs to high-pressure sales talk and forces him
to buy a car on the installment plan. By that time he is so far gone
that one thing more seems no great matter.[14]

What Lytle did not see is that eventually, rural boys not lucky enough
to inherit farms would be driven over those good roads either to a college,
where they would be tutored to leave home forever, or to a military recruiting station, where they would enter the coldwater barracks of Uncle
Sam, who one day would send them halfway around the world to kill and
die for . . . oil to fuel their cars. Good roads led to Kuwait City, or Palo Alto,
or anywhere but home.

So Mr. Lytle's South was invaded yet again, not by Union troops but by
outsiders seeking bucolic pleasures, the Fountain of Youth, and fabled
Florida. And this time, it was the South's fault. In *Dirt Roads to Dixie*
(1991), Howard Lawrence Preston describes how the good-roads gospel
preached by southern politicians—a "network of local roads connecting
isolated hamlets throughout the region with larger towns and market
centers"[15]—was hijacked by New Southrons, whose goals included tour-
ism and bringing in northern industry.

Prior to 1910 only the most intrepid motorist ventured southward, so
poor were the roads and nonexistent were the bridges. "I am satisfied
North Carolina was saved from the invasion of Sherman because the
roads were so bad he could not get through,"[16] said Charlotte mayor
Charles A. Bland in 1902. Bland was a good-roads man, and this was a
strange way to make his case.

But Bland was on to something. Tourist highways became the snake
oil of business-minded southerners, and this was to "prove instrumental
to the emergence of a different South: one that conformed more closely to
national rather than regional standards, and one with a future that
promised prosperity not to farmers but to the business community."[17]
Provincialism was the first casualty of tourist highways. Foreign corre-
spondent Anne O'Hare McCormick observed in 1922, "If anyone de-
serves a government bonus for destroying sectionalism, it is surely the
inventor of the cheap touring car."[18]

Or as A. G. Batchelder of the American Automobile Association told
the North Carolina Good Roads Association in 1912, "a long stretch of improved road . . . changes . . . backward localities into progressive ones."[19]

Among the hoary institutions that needed a makeover were the one-
room schoolhouses in which rural Americans had traditionally been educated. "The success of the consolidated schools," declared Senator William H. Thompson (D-KS) in 1916, "depends almost entirely upon the
condition of the public roads."[20]

"Consolidation of one-room country school houses into high grade central schools is going forward rapidly in [North Carolina]," reported *The*

World's Work in 1922. "It would not be possible without good roads over which the children can be carried in practically all kinds of weather."[21]

The number of children being bused daily to school rose from 875,462 in 1926 to 3,967,411 in 1940. In 1932, an article in *Roads and Streets*, an industry magazine, asserted: "The little red schoolhouse continues its retreat before the motor age. Its rate of disappearance is definitely proportioned to the rate of increase in improved highway mileage. Every acceleration in road construction is marked by a corresponding decrease in the number of one-room schools."[22] (The link was a matter of federal policy: the 1936 secondary federal aid act targeted roads on which rural school buses ran.)

Road progressives made a fetish of mobility. Leaving home, family, and neighbors—whether for the day on a school bus, for the week on a vacation, or forever in a career—was, axiomatically, good. But why? Why? Why?

Before the automobile, "many rural folks spent their whole lives in one location; some never traveled more than fifty miles from home,"[23] a historian noted with pity. Yet travel in and of itself simply substitutes a series of brief and meaningless encounters with strangers and strange places for the solidity (the sodality, the solidarity) of the familiar.

The sociologist Francis E. Merrill would remark at midcentury, "The instability of the family arising from extreme mobility is . . . a social problem. Such institutions as the church, the school, and the agencies of local government undergo a decline in influence in a mobile society."[24]

Merrill's colleagues Walter Firey, Charles P. Loomis, and J. Allan Beegle explained:

> Highways have disrupted the stable localistic groupings that have become the bedrock of America's rural life. Distinctive neighborhood institutions—the church, the lodge, the country schoolhouse—have been succumbing before the competition offered by their urban equivalents. . . . [Lost are] these old-time localistic institutions, with their typically intimate, face-to-face associations, . . . [which were] potent citizen-building forces. . . . Family life itself is changing. The individualization of activities, long so typical of urban family life, is manifesting itself in rural families as well. In place of family picnics, family reunions, and family church-going . . . father goes to the lodge meeting, mother attends the church missionary society meeting, daughter goes to the high school dance, and junior takes in a movie.

(Television, we must concede, has brought everyone back home, at least on Must-See TV Night.)

"Urban patterns," the trio added, "are being borne out along the highways into rural areas to a much greater degree than rural patterns are being borne inward toward the cities."[25] (Which is why cocaine and hip-hop infiltrated the land of hemp and square dancing.)

The citizens of Muncie, Indiana, subjects of Robert S. and Helen Merrell Lynd's *Middletown* (1929), saw it coming. They viewed the automobile and good roads charily. Said one wife:

> In the nineties we were all much more together. People brought chairs and cushions out of the house and sat on the lawn evenings. We rolled out a strip of carpet and put cushions on the porch step to take care of the unlimited overflow of neighbors that dropped by. We'd sit out so all evening. The younger couples perhaps would wander off for half an hour to get a soda but come back to join in the informal singing or listen while somebody strummed a mandolin or guitar.[26]

"What on earth *do* you want me to do? Just sit around home all evening?" whined a "popular high school girl . . . when her father discouraged her going out motoring for the evening with a young blade in a rakish car."[27] We laugh at the innocence of this exchange—she's only going for a ride, dad; do you want her to stay home and bake cookies with a costive mother who looks like Beulah Bondi?—but soon enough the automobile will take her away, for good (or for bad), and though this is her "choice" it is a choice framed for her by government policy. At bottom, good roads is about deracination, about the uprooting of Americans from their home places, and it was Uncle Sam, not free enterprise or the commies, who built these highways to—wherever.

But aren't farm-to-market roads an exception? As Congressman Dorsey W. Shackleford (D-MO), chairman of the House Committee on Roads, insisted: "the proper function of roads is not to connect antipodal oceans nor the distant capitals of far-away States, but to make easy communication between the farms on one hand and the towns and railway stations on the other, to the end that the farmer may market his crops at less expense and the town dweller may get farm products more easily and at less cost."[28] This may be an entirely legitimate activity for local government (though Mr. Lytle begs to differ) but once hinterlands politicians conceded the legitimacy of a national transportation policy—at the very moment when the country was undergoing a frenetic and perhaps irreversible fit of urbanization—they gave the game away.

And then came the War to End All Wars, and it did what wars always do: centralize economic and political power and promote a state-sponsored "progress" that undermines family and community life. In its aftermath, between 1920 and 1927, the secretary of war turned over $225 million of surplus war materials (including 25,000 army trucks), which then were used in highway construction.

In 1900 there had been but 5,000 autos nationwide; come 1910, 458,500 motor vehicles were registered in the various states; and by the 1920s more than half of American families owned a car.

Commerce began deserting small downtowns for the highway-boomed outskirts. In his study of early twentieth-century Oregon, Illinois, geographer Norman T. Moline examined the ways in which improved roads brought a "new scale of distance and time" to the people of one small and relatively self-sufficient town. Automobiles and state-paved highways brought Oregon within the gravitational pull of the city of Rockford, about twenty-five miles away. Despite a "Boost Oregon: Trade at Home" campaign designed to "preserve Oregon not only as a commercial 'place on the map' but, more importantly, as any kind of a place," Rockford's lure proved irresistible.

"We will meet Rockford prices,"[29] pledged one merchant in the *Ogle County Republican* in 1920. The knee-jerk response to this is hurrah: good roads spur competition, and the consumer benefits. But one can also read this as the desperate effort of an Oregon businessman to counter the artificial advantage that government subsidy has given urban companies, which, in the absence of state intervention, would not be plausible competitors. (Plans for private "interurbans," or trolleys to and from Oregon, always came a cropper.)

The *Republican* repined in 1924: "People no longer indulge in old fashioned visits. Everyone has an automobile and no one stays at home long enough to give a fellow a chance to visit them."[30] One destination of roving Oregonians was the theater in Rockford, which was not darkened by blue laws. In 1927 the voters of Oregon chose to permit Sunday movies. Proponents argued, "If Oregon did not have to compete with surrounding towns connected by good roads, then there would be no serious reason for having Sunday pictures here. . . . Oregon's good roads are serving more as an outlet to trade than as an inlet."[31]

A diarist noted on July 4, 1914: "No one in town . . . all to Rockford or Dixon to celebrate."[32] A sad comment, though good roads did make possible intertown athletic competitions, well-attended county fairs, and other wholesome activities. These and a bushel of blessings have been delivered along paths of dirt and gravel and asphalt.

And of course there is a romanticism about the open road, whether in Woody Guthrie's "ribboned highways" or Jack Kerouac's Sal Paradise whooping and yeasaying as he crosses Nebraska in an old jalopy, scattering love and adjectives in his wake. (Kerouac himself hated joyriding. He usually cowered in the backseat, wanting nothing more than a lift home to Lowell.) I, too, ride the roads, and in some ways they have enriched my life. Much has been gained—but tell me, what is lost?

WHY LIKE IKE?

Road building was a relief measure during the New Deal. By 1936, Washington spent more on roads than did all forty-eight states combined. In 1938, 47 percent of WPA personnel were "workin' on the highway." Whatever equilibrium had existed in the federal-state-local relationship was tipped; by the late 1930s, although "local officials directed road construction . . . state and federal engineers increasingly wrote their specifications, supervised their work, and limited their initiatives."[33]

The grand theme of the 1940s was reconstruction; never before had Nathaniel Hawthorne's dictum "the hand that renovates is always more sacrilegious than that which destroys" contained so much truth. In transportation, the attitude was that "if men were going to be put to work on roads after the war, they should construct a different social, urban, and economic order, not just build highways."[34] The outline of a national interstate system had gathered dust in desk drawers for decades—the AAA had long lobbied for a federal takeover of important state highways—and in wartime, when the country seemed so malleable, FDR's Interregional Highway Committee recommended (in 1944) the creation of a 41,000-mile interstate. (Rexford G. Tugwell was a committee member. The cast of villains never changes, does it?) Farmers and New Englanders remained skeptical, for the usual reasons; the U.S. Chamber of Commerce backed federal sponsorship of this network, while one of its spokesmen denounced rural agitation for farm-to-market roads as "just plain national socialism."[35]

But the interstate was to be a mere gleam in New Dealers' eyes—until the Republican sugar daddies showed up. "America lives on wheels, and we have to provide the highways to keep America living on wheels and keep the kind and form of life that we want,"[36] declaimed Secretary of the Treasury George M. Humphrey in May 1955. Humphrey was the house skinflint of the Eisenhower administration, but when the sound of earthmovers and smell of pavement filled the air, he and his boss became as giddy as teenaged girls contemplating Ricky Nelson.

President Eisenhower had been much impressed by Hitler's autobahn. Half a world and most of a lifetime removed from his native Abilene, Kansas, Ike thought that automobiles meant "greater happiness,"[37] and to spread joy throughout the kingdom he delegated to soldiers cum bureaucrats, such as Generals Lucius D. Clay and John H. Bragdon, the conception of an American autobahn. After a false start in 1955, and several months of haggling over financing details in early 1956, on June 29, 1956, the president signed the legislation creating the National System of Interstate and Defense Highways. Ninety percent of the construction costs were to be paid by the federal government out of a Highway Trust Fund that was fed by taxes on parts, accessories, fuel, and trucks.

This colossal project, 41,000 miles plus, was to be the "greatest public works project in history," as administration spokesmen often boasted. Despite being sold as a "capitalistic milestone," it was in fact "a quasi-socialistic program that would transform America forever."[38] As with good roads, no one, apart from a few lonely poets and radicals, found fault with a grandiose plan that would do more to uproot the American people than any other policy save war and conscription.

"Everyone agrees that the new highways are needed,"[39] editorialized *The New Republic*, and even the Eisenhower administration's tightwad nemesis, Senate Finance Committee chairman Harry F. Byrd (D-VA), was careful to tell his colleagues that "my objections to this proposal do not come from . . . a lack of appreciation of the need for very substantial sums for road improvements."[40] Instead, Byrd urged the continuation of the federal-aid system of matching grants ($500 million annually by the 1950s) and the repeal of the federal gas tax, to be reimposed by the states—a modest step in a federalist direction, to be sure, but hardly a stand for the ages.

American conservatives were silent on the matter. There was a Cold War being waged, and the transformation of American life was of far less consequence to editors of the *National Review* than, say, CIA estimates of the annual requisitioning of pencils within the Warsaw Pact. For dissent, one had to look to independent literary men of the Left: Lewis Mumford, Paul Goodman, Richard Wilbur. David Cort naysayed in *The Nation:*

This estrangement of the American family by gigantism may be the clue to the whole automobile problem. It may often be just this estrangement that gives the family head the compulsion to buy a car. His car identifies him with the gigantism. It is his car, his bum carburetor, a few individual dents and some interior litter. When he rides out into the maelstrom, he reestablishes his part in the huge thing rushing past his door. This compels the civilization to build yet more gigantic highways and the citizen feels worse again.

The family drives out to visit Aunt Esther in Hempstead, whom they don't like, instead of dropping around the corner to see Aunt Myrtle, whom they do like; or to a restaurant twenty miles away that is worse than the one down two blocks. The real purpose of the trips is to get into the maelstrom, which they all pretend to hate.[41]

General Bragdon claimed that the Interstate would be "a continuous stabilizing force,"[42] but for what? The president told a meeting of Senate and House members on February 21, 1955, that a massive road program was "vitally essential for national defense" and would "help the steel and auto spare parts industry."[43] And to Eisenhower, with his long residences in Europe, New York City, and Washington, wasn't that the sum of America?

The war and highway industries have been locked in an embrace since the First World War, and never was it tighter than in the early years of the Interstate—and Defense, remember—system. Eisenhower's secretary of defense, Charles Wilson, came from General Motors; JFK's man in the Pentagon, Robert McNamara, rolled off the Ford line. The Interstate was eulogized "as vital a part of our arsenal as are weapons and planes,"[44] in *Nation's Business*.

"A safe and efficient highway network is essential to America's military and civil defense, and to the economy,"[45] averred the Clay committee in 1955. (American families and towns merited not even an afterthought.) This absurdity reached its acme in a 1969 publication of the Highway Users Conference, which assured motorists that when the big one drops, the car becomes "a rolling home. . . . Persons can eat and sleep in it, keep warm and dry, receive instructions by radio, drive out of danger areas, and even be afforded some protection against nuclear fallout."[46] (You'd be better off praying for Mad Max to show up.)

WE'RE ON THE ROAD TO NOWHERE

In "A Car-Traveling People (1955)," a pamphlet of the Automobile Manufacturer's Association, the inappropriately surnamed Franklin M. Reck wrote:

> Open-country churches, one-room schools, and crossroads stores are boarded up and abandoned. . . . At the turn of the century, Main Street was crowded on the Fourth of July. Flags flying, a parade, and fireworks in the park. The celebration had to be in town because it was so hard to go anywhere. . . . Today, Main Street is deserted on the Fourth. The folks are all out in the country with their kids.[47]

And this was from a publicist for the auto industry!

Mr. Reck hailed the salubriousness of the highway revolution. "By 1942 the automobile had completed its transformation of medical practice . . . Nearly half the doctors in small villages have disappeared because they're no longer needed. Many small, poorly equipped hospitals have closed up in favor of better hospitals in nearby larger towns."[48] Those of us who are ministered to in these larger town hospitals are grateful, though left out of the calculus are the baneful effects of the doctor dearth in small towns—and the hospital beds and cemetery plots that automobile accidents fill each year.

Reck concluded: "The surfaced highway and the car have centralized farm living. Fewer and better stores. Fewer and better schools. Fewer and better hospitals."[49] Fewer and better lives, he might have added.

"People in motion" may have been glamorized by a hippie pop song of the 1960s, but they were set in motion some years earlier. In its 1964 report, *Highways and Economic and Social Changes*, the U.S. Department of Commerce noted that 34 million people—one-fifth of the population at that time—changed residence each year. These "population transfers [including the migration of rural southern blacks into northern cities] could not have been made adequately without [highways]."[50] Indeed, an authorized history of the moving and storage industry allows that "there is no question that the [Interstate] highway system has revolutionized both the mode and the quantity of long-distance American travel and general mobility."[51]

In the sticks, the Department of Commerce reported, "the conversion of farm land to other uses ordinarily occurs first near the interchange points of limited access highways."[52] Again, this is not the wild charge of some dreamy arcadian, pining away in his cabin for an agrestic utopia which never existed, but a simple statement of fact: this development, this de-rustication, was a result of government policy.

By and large, American conservatives defended the highway system and the automobile from the long-haired lackbeards who were questioning such hallowed institutions as the Pentagon, the state university, and General Motors. B. Bruce-Briggs's lively *The War Against the Automobile* (1977) counterpunched the footsore nags and Naderites. Bruce-Briggs cooed over "our present system" of transportation, which meets our needs beautifully "even though nobody really planned it. It just worked out that way through the myriad individual decisions of hundreds of millions of people."[53]

It just worked out that way. Oh, really? Describing the evolution of U.S. highway policy in Misesian language is like praising Mr. and Mrs. Jackson for Michael's current appearance. The invisible hand did not build the Interstate.

Bruce-Briggs ascribes the autophobia of the 1960s and 1970s to New Class elitists, and there is a certain truth in it; some of these people were collectivists who wished to herd the urban working classes into mass transit, thus creating a nation of straphanging proles and depriving ordinary Americans of the feeling of independence—illusory or not—that a car can give.

Then there was the beside-the-point obsession with billboards. Lady Bird Johnson chirped to the White House Council on Natural Beauty in May 1965, "Our immediate problem is: How can one best fight ugliness in a nation such as ours—where there is great freedom of action or inaction for every individual and every interest—where there is virtually no artistic control?"[54] The obscenity here is staggering: as Lady Bird twittered on about billboards (most of which advertise small local motels and restaurants), her husband, no paragon of Natural Beauty himself, was consigning hundreds of thousands of Americans and Vietnamese to grisly deaths.

By this time a few of the sharper liberals, notably Senator Eugene McCarthy (D-MN), had begun to question the wisdom of having Uncle Sam pave till we drop. Even Hubert Horatio Humphrey, the Happy Warrior of Bloated Liberalism, the Most Voluble Player of Tired Liberal Clichés, observed:

> This is a peculiar time. People who live in the cities work in the country and people who live in the country work in the cities. Many of the industrial workers in the Twin City area live in the center of the city and work 30 miles out of town. The bankers, stockbrokers, insurance salesmen, and the real estate agents live 30 miles out in the country and work in town. The automobile has done this. We have permitted ourselves to be victims of four wheels with a 400 horsepower motor at a time when we shouldn't require four wheels for every trip.[55]

The building orgy had inflated land values along nonurban routes, making home buying an impossible proposition for some natives and turning formerly autonomous towns with characters all their own into mere bedroom communities, where transients sleep in pricey flophouses. More than 40,000 Americans are killed on the highways each year—and how many towns, how many Oregon, Illinoises, have died their own slow deaths?

THIS LAND IS MY LAND

In a lyrical *Audobon* look at Ike's autobahn, John G. Mitchell imagined the Interstate haunted by the ghosts of the displaced:

> Just once did I bat an eye at one of them from the window of a passing car? That one there, sitting in my imagination in his summer undershirt, on the front stoop. What was his name? How long had he lived here when they broke the news to him—a map on page one of the *Post*, the dotted line impaling his neighborhood? Then the knock at the door and the talk of appraisal. Not this house! he said. He had lived here all his life and they would have to bury him with their bulldozers. But in the end, he moved. Hundreds moved. Across the country, through three decades of right-of-way acquisition, *hundreds of thousands* moved. It was all for the greater good, they

were told. It was for America. Ask not what you can do for your country, just get out of our way.[56]

That 1964 U.S. Department of Commerce publication showed real insight: "People living in the right-of-way path of a planned highway have the problem of finding other places to live." Well, yes. When the government condemns *your* property, forces you off *your* land, at gunpoint in some piquant instances, it does present a small "problem." "The inconvenience is unavoidable,"[57] the DOC opined, which is flatly untrue—if the highway is not built, there's plenty of convenience all around.

But don't despair, displaced ones. The Commerce flacks assured us that very often "when a resident changes his old home for a new dwelling place"—that is, when the cops and bulldozers chase a family from their home—"living conditions" are "improved."[58] (Photographs of the homes of lucky Californians who had been "relocated"—and whose new dwellings had higher assessments than their old rattraps—were helpfully included. These are as convincing as the before and after photos in supermarket tabloids which show us a frowning frump, who, in six short weeks, with the aid of a few pills, becomes a dead ringer for Sharon Stone.)

The devastation that highway construction and urban renewal visited upon cities has been memorably chronicled by Jane Jacobs, A. Q. Mowbray, and others. The architects of U.S. transportation policy expected, even welcomed, the ruin. In 1939, Studebaker president Paul Hoffman insouciantly spoke of "gashing our way ruthlessly through built-up sections of overcrowded cities"[59]; a quarter-century later the egregious Robert Moses admitted that "in an overbuilt metropolis you have to hack your way with a meat ax."[60]

By the late 1960s, the Interstate and Defense Highway System was displacing 57,000 people per year. Moses's meat ax was getting quite a workout. (Euphemism was by now the official language of government—displacements at home, body counts and kill ratios abroad.) Eighty-seven percent of the buildings fed to the Highway Moloch were residences. Between 1947 and 1969, 98,000 homes were razed in California alone. These were often modest abodes, though be they ever so humble, there's no place like home. And there is no experience quite so shattering as being homeless.

One woman told A. Q. Mowbray after she, her husband, and their retarded daughter were forced to leave Lee Street in Philadelphia to make way for the Delaware Expressway: "Every time I think or talk about [Lee Street], it makes me cry. It was a shame to make us move." Her husband "comes home and just sits in his chair. He doesn't try to get out and socialize with the people on the block, like he did in our old house."[61] Some elderly neighbors died in the awful interim between receiving the condemnation notice and the sinister swing of the wrecking ball.

The dispossessed were often urban blacks. As the embers of riot settled on Newark, New Jersey, LBJ advisor Daniel Patrick Moynihan received a letter from several Newark citizens that read, in part, "They are tearing down our homes and building up medical colleges and motor clubs and parking lots and we need decent private homes to live in. They are tearing down our best schools and churches to build a highway. We are over here in provity [sic] and bondage. There are [sic] supposed to be justice for all. Where are that justice?"[62]

Where, indeed? "This will stop the freeways,"[63] said a black defender of his neighborhood in Washington, D.C., holding up a book of matches, but fire could not melt the icy resolve of the highwaymen to bulldoze those human nuisances who blocked the path of progress. A band of black militants calling themselves "Niggers Incorporated" demanded, "No more white highways through black bedrooms"[64]; the group's chairman urged his people to "take up arms to defend their neighborhoods."[65] It is all very easy to tut-tut when the poor resort to threats of violence to keep the state from paving over the hearthstone, but what else could they do? Niggers Incorporated is nothing compared to Exxon, General Motors, and the Association of General Contractors.

Besides, was any member of Niggers Incorporated a Certified Expert? In 1968 the president of the unfortunately acronymed AASHO (American Association of State Highway Officials) warned a congressional committee that "to allow local people to have a greater voice in the highway location and design for which they are not trained would negate the experience of trained highway professionals."[66] This is the logic of progressivism, and only a radical or reactionary could disagree.

"It is not our desire to stand in the way of progress," freeway foes often prefaced their case, thus conceding the game before the opening kickoff. Partisans of progress have been canny: they write the rules, rig the game, pay the umpires, and call their victory inevitable. Those losers indecorous enough to complain are socialists or hippies or white trash or niggers, incorporated or not.

But this a lie, and though the game is long over we can at least insist on a fair accounting. The expressways that deface our beautiful country, that carry our children far from home, that destroyed hundreds of thousands of lives, that poison the air that we breathe—that carry hypocrites like me to the University of Rochester library so I can write this chapter biting the hand that conveys me—these are monuments not to capitalism or human action or mechanical genius but to the Leviathan State, whose architects wanted a rootless and hypermobile population. And that's exactly what they got.

"To stay at home is best,"[67] said Henry Wadsworth Longfellow. The poet loved to travel in Europe, and even most stick-in-the-muds enjoy a ride to the next town, but in all our going and coming, our cruising along the straight pathways our government has made for us, our transit over the blue-shielded highways that crisscross America like broken blood vessels on a drunk's nose, just where, exactly, did home go?

NOTES

1. William Blake, "The Marriage of Heaven and Hell," *Poems of William Blake* (New York: Crowell, 1964), p. 112.

2. Theodore H. White, "Where Are Those New Roads?" *Collier's*, January 6, 1956; reprinted in *American Highways Today*, ed. by Poyntz Tyler (New York: H. W. Wilson, 1957), p. 138.

3. Hillaire Belloc, *The Road* (New York: Harper & Brothers, 1939), p. 2.

4. Charles L. Dearing, *American Highway Policy* (Washington, D.C.: Brookings Institution, 1941), p. 2.

5. Ibid., p. 43.

6. Ibid., p. 220.

7. Ibid., p. 259.

8. Howard Lawrence Preston, *Dirt Roads to Dixie: Accessibility and Modernization in the South, 1885–1935* (Knoxville: University of Tennessee Press, 1991), pp. 65–66.

9. Ibid., p. 67.

10. Quoted in Dearing, p. 235.

11. Preston, p. 15.

12. Ibid., p. 67.

13. Sinclair Lewis, *The Man Who Knew Coolidge* (New York: Harcourt, Brace and Company, 1928), pp. 234–35.

14. Andrew Lytle, "The Hind Tit," in *I'll Take My Stand* (Baton Rouge: Louisiana State University Press, 1977/1930), pp. 234–37.

15. Preston, p. 6.

16. Ibid., p. 11.

17. Ibid., p. 95.

18. Quoted in Christy Borth, *Mankind on the Move: The Story of Highways* (Washington, D.C.: Automotive Safety Foundation, 1969), p. 224.

19. Ibid., pp. 49–50.

20. Quoted in Dearing, p. 240.

21. Quoted in Preston, p. 161.

22. Ibid.

23. Reynold M. Wik, "The Early Automobile and the American Farmer," in *The Automobile and American Culture*, ed. David L. Lewis and Laurence Goldstein (Ann Arbor: University of Michigan, 1983), p. 37.

24. Francis E. Merrill, "The Highway and Social Problems," in *Highways in Our National Life*, ed. Jean Labatut and Wheaton J. Lane (New York: Arno, 1972/1950), p. 143.

25. Walter Firey, Charles P. Loomis, and J. Allan Beegle, "The Fusion of Urban and Rural," in *Highways in Our National Life*, pp. 160–61.

26. Robert S. Lynd and Helen Merrell Lynd, *Middletown* (New York: Harcourt, Brace and Company, 1929), p. 257.

27. Ibid. The automobile has long been hymned for its romantic possibilities, and while the author is all in favor of young love, the Lynds point out that of the thirty girls hauled into juvenile court for "sex crimes" in a twelve-month period in 1923–24, nineteen did it in an automobile.

28. Quoted in Dearing, p. 81.

29. Norman T. Moline, *Mobility and the Small Town* (Chicago: University of Chicago, Department of Geography, 1971), p. 127.

30. Ibid., p. 100.

31. Ibid., p. 104.

32. Ibid., p. 106.

33. Mark H. Rose, *Interstate: Express Highway Politics 1941–1956* (Lawrence: Regents Press of Kansas, 1979), p. 9.

34. Ibid., p. 17.

35. Ibid., p. 40.

36. Ibid., p. 69.

37. Ibid., p. 70.

38. Stephen B. Goddard, *Getting There: The Epic Struggle between Road and Rail in the American Century* (New York: Basic Books, 1994), p. 184.

39. "Construction Ahead," *The New Republic*, May 16, 1955, p. 5.

40. "Senator Harry F. Byrd," *Congressional Digest* (May 1955): 145.

41. David Cort, "Our Strangling Highways," *The Nation*, April 28, 1955; reprinted in *American Highways Today*, p. 91.

42. Rose, p. 75.

43. Ibid., p. 78.

44. Charles B. Seib, "New Roads: Changed Business Pattern Ahead," *Nation's Business*, July 1956; reprinted in *American Highways Today*, p. 187. For more on the incredible interlocking directorate of the highway-defense complex, see David J. St. Clair, *The Motorization of American Cities* (New York: Praeger, 1986), pp. 137–43.

45. Quoted in Borth, p. 246.

46. Quoted in Ben Kelley, *The Pavers and the Paved* (New York: Donald W. Brown, 1971), p. 10.

47. Franklin M. Reck, "A Car-Traveling People," in *American Highways Today*, p. 29.

48. Ibid., p. 33.

49. Ibid., p. 38.

50. *Highways and Economic and Social Changes* (Washington, D.C.: U.S. Department of Commerce, 1964), p. 67.

51. John Hess, *The Mobile Society: A History of the Moving and Storage Industry* (New York: McGraw-Hill, 1973), pp. 103–4.

52. *Highways and Economic and Social Changes*, p. 131.

53. B. Bruce-Briggs, *The War Against the Automobile* (New York: Dutton, 1977), p. 8.

54. Quoted in John Robinson, *Highways and Our Environment* (New York: McGraw-Hill, 1971), p. 270.

55. Quoted in Bruce-Briggs, p. 19.

56. John G. Mitchell, "30 Years on Ike's Autobahns," *Audobon*, November 1986, pp. 80–81.

57. *Highways and Economic and Social Changes*, p. 111.

58. Ibid., pp. 111–12.

59. Quoted in St. Clair, p. 122.

60. Ibid., p. 152.

61. A. Q. Mowbray, *Road to Ruin* (Philadelphia: Lippincott, 1969), p. 47.

62. Ibid., pp. 34–35.

63. Ibid., p. 177.

64. Ibid., p. 224.

65. Ibid., p. 227.

66. Quoted in Kelley, p. 129.

67. Henry Wadsworth Longfellow, "Song," *The Complete Poetical Works of Henry Wadsworth Longfellow* (Cambridge, Mass.: Houghton, Mifflin and Company, 1893), pp. 340–41.

6

Doesn't Anybody Stay in One Country Anymore? Uncle Sam Wants You—to Move

In 1996 I interviewed former secretary of defense Caspar Weinberger, and earned his glare when I asked if the U.S. military wasn't "a government-subsidized uprooting of the population." My cointerviewer affably chided me for being a wise guy, but I was dead serious: the single greatest cause of American rootlessness over the last half century has been our standing army. (If it really were standing it wouldn't be so bad: alas, it never stops moving.)

To vocalize such heresy within the Beltway is akin to walking up K Street wearing a sandwich board reading, "I'm a Nut." Never mind that our forbears would ask the same question. James Madison, in his notes on the Constitutional Convention of 1787, casually remarked that "armies in time of peace are allowed on all hands to be an evil."[1] Benjamin Rush, Declaration signatory and later President Adams's treasurer of the U.S. Mint, proposed in 1792 that two mottoes be painted "over the portals of the Department of War": "An office for butchering the human species" and "A Widow and Orphan making office."[2] I don't suppose Cap would have gone for that.

Simply put, maintenance of a large standing army, especially an army in which men are stationed away from that place which they and their families call "home," is a significant factor in the destruction of American family life. Those who support a large standing army do more to undermine American families than do most of the exotic bogeymen of "family-values" propaganda.

The militia, which served as the core of the Revolutionary Army, was "purely a local and defensive force."[3] The father of modern political science, William H. Riker, wrote, "The basis of organization was almost invariably territorial"[4]: men trained with their neighbors to defend their homes and families against invasion. When the eccentric Anti-Federalist toper Luther Martin of Maryland asked his fellow delegates to the Constitutional Convention whether an overreaching Congress might someday order "the *whole* militia of Maryland to the *remotest* part of the Union,"[5] he was assured that such an outlandish thing could never happen.

Like most irresponsible fear-mongers, Luther was on to something. The spurious version of the militia known as the National Guard, which was vitalized in the Gilded Age largely to break strikes, succeeded only because "the traditional system of geographical enrollment," under which "units would have contained men in sympathy with the strikers and would not therefore have been trustworthy"[6] strike-breakers, was no longer in effect. Any fantasy that National Guard units were congregations of neighbors joined together in defense of their home states was shattered in the 1980s, when the Reagan administration overrode the objections of several governors, including Michael Dukakis of Massachusetts, and ordered, putatively, state guards to board the banana boat to Central America.

IT WAS A VERY GOOD WAR

"National defense," a hyperelastic and, thus, meaningless term, has elevated rootlessness to a virtue.

Take the Second World War. Quite apart from its role in centralizing political power, enfeebling regional culture, and creating hundreds of thousands of widows and orphans, the "Good War" scattered Americans like so many deuces in a bottomless deck of cards. A Bureau of the Census report remarked in 1945, "Never before in the history of our country has there been so great a shuffling and redistribution of population in so short a time."[7] More than 15 million Americans, or 12 percent of the civilian population, resided in a different county in March 1945 than they had on December 7, 1941—and this doesn't even count the 12 million-plus who were wearing Uncle Sam's khaki. Twenty-seven million migrants—and unlike the Okie Joads, who at least traveled as an extended family, these wartime wayfarers were severed, sometimes forever, from the family tree. (Twelve million moved permanently to another state.)

Sociologist Francis E. Merrill wrote in 1950, "The process of reshuffling millions of workers, much of it carried out on the highways of the nation, was accomplished with the tacit approval of all concerned. The dislocation in the personal lives of the mobile persons was largely overlooked or, when considered at all, was viewed as an unfortunate but unavoidable concomitant of total mobilization."[8]

Bad habits are hard to break: in the fourteen months following the war, more than 10 million civilians changed their county of residence at least once, the majority for job-related reasons. Today, one-third of all

Americans live outside their natal state. Twelve states are afflicted with
a majority of immigrants, most fantastically Nevada, wherein almost 80
percent were born elsewhere. No doubt there are things to be said for
Bugsy Siegel, Steve Wynn, and the Mustang Ranch, but do we want all of
America to look like Las Vegas?

The novelist John P. Marquand calculated the war's cost in homey
terms: "There was no use thinking any longer that someone who belonged to you might live in your house after you were through with it."[9]

This discontinuity was especially pronounced in the southern and border states. Between 1940 and 1945 the farm population declined from
30.5 million to 24.4 million; the yellow brick road was crowded with hicks
lured by the siren song emanating from the defense plants in the industrial Midwest and California. (The federal government supplied 90 percent of California's new investment capital during the war; its
population increased by 53 percent over the decade.) One-fifth of the
South's rural population left during the war years: one joke had it that
America lost three states in the early 1940s: "Kentucky and Tennessee
had gone to Indiana, and Indiana had gone to hell."[10] Too few migrants
displayed the good sense of one David Crockett Lee, who said: "We found
Detroit a cold city, a city without a heart or a soul. So we are going back to
Tennessee."[11]

"There is perhaps no aspect of family life unaffected by the war,"[12] declared social historian Richard Polenberg. For five or six years children
grew up without fathers and wives made do without husbands. In 1943
the Selective Service began to induct fathers, and "by V-J Day, of the
6,200,000 classified fathers aged 18 to 37, one-fifth were in the service; of
the youngest fathers, aged 18 to 25, more than half (58.2 percent) were on
active duty."[13]

Social worker Josephine D. Abbott fretted in 1943:

> Parental supervision has decreased throughout the United States
> with increased opportunities for mothers to enter war industries
> and for those in the higher socio-economic brackets to engage in the
> war effort. 'Door-key' children are too often the victims of these mis-
> guided parents. In some areas women . . . [are] rejecting and repudi-
> ating their children in their newly found freedom. The high wages
> they now earn gives them a chance to lead a life more exciting than
> that of child bearing and rearing.[14]

(The divorce rate "more than doubled between 1940 and 1946; by 1950
one million veterans had been divorced."[15] Absence may make the heart
grow fonder, but love requires presence above all.)

Mrs. J. Russell Henderson, chairman of the Youth Advisory Association of the Arkansas Council for Social Agencies, complained, "This war

is directly responsible for the boom in badness because children's fathers go off to war and their mothers go to work, and thus the interest of parents is diverted from the home and the children."[16]

Agnes E. Meyer, wife of the *Washington Post* publisher, concurred. After a nationwide tour in 1943 she wrote, "From Buffalo to Wichita, it is the children who are suffering most from mass migration, easy money, unaccustomed hours of work, and the fact that mama has become a welder on the graveyard shift."[17]

The day-care industry was one illegitimate offspring of the grotesque coupling of deserted war wives and that old cuckold-maker Uncle Sam. The Lanham Act of 1940 allocated $50 million for the supervision of Rosie the Riveter's children; at its peak in July 1944, the act was subsidizing 3,102 day-care centers incarcerating 129,357 children. Between 550,000 and 600,000 kids were turned over to Lanham centers during the course of the war.

War-contorted California had 7 percent of the nation's population but "nearly one-quarter of the total number of children enrolled in federally funded child care centers in July 1945."[18] After the war, the Golden State became the harbinger of the day-care revolution; in 1946, the California legislature voted to continue the program, largely due to lobbying from Lanham-created "child care workers" and "clients who had grown reliant on subsidized child care."[19] Though by 1945 women constituted more than a third of the civilian labor force, many resisted the proferred day care, for as a government official conceded, "There is a positive aversion to group care of children in the minds of working women. To some it connotes an inability to care for one's own; to some it has a vague incompatibility with the traditional idea of the American home; to others it has a taint of socialism."[20]

Father's absence, sometimes permanent, ruptured families, and into this breach slipped the U.S. government. This was nothing new. The explosive growth of the nation's military pension system in the years following the Civil War has been called the federal government's first family policy; "by 1893, over 40 percent of the federal budget went to support widows, orphans, the elderly, and invalid soldiers."[21] Surely recompense was one motive for these alms, but another reason for generous pensions was "to increase the number of men willing to leave their families."[22]

In his study of 135 war-broken Iowa families in the 1940s, Reuben Hill noted that all was not bleakness and loss:

> On the one hand is the family where husband, wife, and children before induction were inseparable, did all their family planning together, and took all their recreation as a group. For them the absence of the husband left an aching void which could be filled only by his return. On the other hand we see a family which for years

suffered neglect from a drinking, philandering husband, in which there was never any assurance how much of a pay check would arrive home. For them the fact of the father's absence was a relief and the security of the allotment checks was doubly appreciated.[23]

Uncle Sam was the compleat adulterer: after booting shiftless dad from the home, he sent mom regular checks and didn't even strew dirty socks about the bedroom.

Even in families where father was preferred to a government check, reunion was fraught with problems. Families had become female-centered, and the revenant father was sometimes regarded as an interloper. Moreover, the "lack of responsibility in army life"[24] had ill-equipped men used to taking orders to be fathers again. Reuben Hill found that large families suffered most from war. "The larger the family when the husband left for service, the poorer the adjustment to his departure on the part of his loved ones," for "children are burdensome" and "introduce complications which appear to worsen family adjustments to crises of separation and reunion."[25]

Whole communities were ravaged, irrevocably, by the wartime dislocations. Boomtowns sprung up around defense industries and military bases, burying towns under a manswarm of displaced persons. Don Johnson of Flint, Michigan, was to say years later:

> One of the biggest impacts the war had was to create a much more mobile society. As a result we have people who are not tied into the community structure in the same way they were before. They don't have the same sense of obligation to each other, or to the community. . . . Somehow, as a society, we have never gone back to the prewar values of family, friends, church and community.[26]

The Willow Run, Michigan, Ford plant employed 42,000 persons, most from southerly climes; the migrants "took little if any part in the religious, political and social life of the community."[27] The adjustment made the poor whites of Kentucky and Tennessee into something that their ancestors would not have recognized, for factory life was "foreign to much of the older mountain culture, where time was marked by seasonal change, important events, and the length of shadows."[28] They learned to punch a clock—but not hard enough to break it. Meanwhile, between December 1941 and July 1943, 6,000 small businesses in Arkansas had to close because of labor shortages—the boys were overseas and the hardscrabble families had gone north.

Military bases brought venereal disease, economic disruption, and land theft to the outlands. (Seasoned wankers still know that the best peep shows are found adjacent to military bases.)

Among the cities transmogrified by militarism was Geneva, New York, a small Finger Lakes city of gracious porticoes and Episcopalian niceties, which was decimated when 45,000 transients bunked at nearby Sampson naval training center. The stately old homes were hastily remodeled into apartments; wooden barracks were thrown up to catch the "human avalanche." As local historian Arch Merrill wrote, "a blue tide surged into Geneva every night. The city virtually became a roaring Navy camp and the blare of the juke boxes in the 20 night spots all but drowned out the thunder of the organ of Trinity Church and the voices of the traditional past."[29]

The city became a military dependent. Rouged and slinky, she had a fat purse for several years, as the Cold War kept Sampson a Goliath. But the base closed in 1956, when Uncle Sam fled the Northeast for the Sun Belt, and Geneva has yet really to recover.

MOVE IT! MOVE IT! MOVE IT!

During Senate hearings in 1945 on the ratification of the Charter of the United Nations, Mrs. Cecil Norton Broy, representing a ladies' study club of Arlington, Virginia, cautioned the senators against

> the further disruption of normal American family life. . . . Our men would be like hired mercenary soldiers going forth to protect the commercial interests of greed and power. Our men thus forced into foreign service would see little if any of their native soil again. We would be working on the principle of scattering the most virile of our men over the face of the globe.[30]

As the Good War segued into the Cold War, that is exactly what happened. As one weary woman told an oral historian,

> It seems as if all my life I have been waiting for men to return from war.
>   In the '40s my uncles.
>   In the '50s my college friends. Some did not return.
>   In the '60s I waited for my husband to return from two tours in Viet Nam.[31]

Ninety percent of the 50,000–plus Americans who died in Vietnam were twenty-six years of age or younger; more than 2.5 million American men served in Vietnam, "away from families and from the arena of normal courtship activities."[32] Paying five bucks to a Saigon prostitute is no substitute for taking the girl next door to the harvest moon dance. In 1971, E. James Lieberman of the Harvard School of Public Health wondered if the Cold War–induced "migration of men away from their families" might explain "the striking increase in the percentage of single young women in the population between 1960 and 1969."[33]

Anyone who complained that fathers and mothers were being ripped from their homeplaces and fed to Moloch was a malcontent, or, in the parlance of the playground bully, a *baby*. Nancy Shea, consort of an Army major and author of *The Army Wife*, told the widows-in-training in 1941:

> When a young woman asks herself, 'Shall I like Army life?' the answer depends solely upon her individual tastes. If she is a spoiled "mama girl," and cannot bear to be separated from her girlhood friends and home, then she won't like Army life. If she enjoys travel, a life in which one moves often and sometimes on a few hours' notice, and is able to adjust herself to conditions and take whatever comes with a smile, then she will be happy![34]

(Shea's book counsels such utter self-effacement, such a perversion of healthy family life, that no woman with spirit could read it and do anything but toss it across the room and tear into a chorus of "I am Woman/Hear me Roar.")

An official history of the moving and storage industry affirms the cause and effect of "the United States' involvement in World War II and the formation of the thousands of interstate household goods carriers."[35] David Brosky, an industry lawyer, averred, "Following the War, the stationing of large military forces overseas produced a dramatic impact on the whole business of shipping household goods. The decision to have Mrs. GI Joe join her husband overseas and establish a reasonable facsimile of her American home abroad had a revolutionary impact on the industry"[36]—as well as on Mr. and Mrs. GI Joe and children, one might add.

The veterans of the 1940s became the organization men of the 1950s: "periodic transfer . . . is a positive good in itself,"[37] as forward-looking future-oriented big-business managers came to believe. Relocation was de rigueur within the IBM culture. "We never plan to transfer," one company president told William Whyte, "and we never *make* a man move. Of course, he kills his career if he doesn't. But we never *make* him do it."[38]

Well, the military certainly *makes* him do it. Yes, other occupations keep the moving vans rolling, but "none are so predictably mobile as the three- to four-year military tour of duty," which, as Ellwyn R. Stoddard writes, "alienates [the military wife] from civilian involvement and 'community roots' for her and family members."[39] A typical study of a military apartment complex in the South found that half of its five hundred families had been there less than a year; "the community turns over almost completely every three years."[40]

For our military families, the consequences can be devastating. "Mobility is associated with psychiatric casualty rates among both adults and children,"[41] wrote two researchers at the Walter Reed General Hospital in 1964. And no employer demands constant movement quite like the U.S. military.

"If Uncle Sam wanted you to have a wife, he'd have issued you one," went one (now hopelessly anachronistic) military aphorism. Before Vietnam, most military personnel were single; by 1973, more than 80 percent of Army officers were married, and the single man's army was history. Forests of research indicate that "women feel that constant mobility is detrimental to their marital relationships"[42]; even the most devoted couple can stumble when there's nothing under their feet.

In her study "Separation and Female Centeredness in the Military Family," Janice G. Rienerth wrote, "The stressful effects of U.S. geographic mobility have been underestimated; moving often places inordinate demands on the individual to adapt and raises continued challenges to identity. In moving, the only seasoned relationship the wife takes with her is that of the nuclear family." When her man is at sea, or on maneuvers, or anywhere but home, the wife cannot rely on the usual support systems of kin and neighbors: there are only other military families, who are liable to vanish just as friendships are being formed. The result is "the development of a family type independent of the father."[43] (Even tearful and long-prayed-for reunions can't overcome the debilitating effects of separation: 30 percent of Vietnamese POW marriages failed within a year of the husband's return.)[44]

The waiting is the hardest part. In her study of naval families in Tidewater, Virginia, Kathryn Brown Decker noted "the presence of depressive symptoms"[45]—crying, aggressive behavior, resentment—in children whose fathers were at sea. The major events that we call "little things"—Daddy missing Susie's birthday, his anniversary, Christmas—tormented the naval wives, who were learning that the military is a harsh mistress.

Seemingly every American this side of Toni Morrison deplores the absence of fathers in the black community, but not a peep is raised if the absent dad has medals pinned to his chest. A classic study of the children of Norwegian sailors found that "the father-separated boys, insecure in their masculinity, struggled to resemble the father but reacted with compensatory masculine bravado,"[46] and four decades of research has yet to contradict this. And what of the simple human cost of lost love?

A 1944 study of delinquent boys with family members over there included an eleven-year-old whose adored eighteen-year-old brother was off to war. When a psychiatrist mentioned the older brother's name, the boy sat with tears streaming down his face, utterly lost in his misery. He gave the impression of being in a depressed state, was unable to answer questions or say anything, and kept on weeping for several minutes. When he finally dried his tears, he said simply that his brother had gone into the army. When the psychiatrist commented that he liked his brother very much, the boy began to cry again.[47]

The inconsolable grief of loss. Multiply this by many millions, and ask what this ocean of tears is for?

James H. S. Bossard likened the removal of a family member to "an amputation." Father's departure means the loss "of the chief disciplinarian, or chief counselor, or both. The removal of an older brother may take away the chief confidant and trail blazer; a sister's absence may mean the loss of a buddy-at-arms."[48]

All too soon we lose our loved ones, one by one, to natural causes; why must the government we finance hasten these losses?

CAN'T SAY BABY WHERE I'LL BE IN A YEAR

We have, over the last fifty years, created a class of citizens, affectionately known as military brats, who are homeless children whose only experience of American life comes from a series of temporary residences on the socialist reservations known as military bases. (Almost alone among political figures, Senator Patrick Moynihan has asked aloud, in what sense the children of U.S. servicemen resident on foreign bases are "American.")

In *Military Brats*, Mary Edwards Wertsch wrote:

There are two questions one can pose that reveal rootlessness as instantly as a litmus test.

The first: *Where are you from?* Military brats do not relish the "where from" question and go through life vainly trying to parry it. Some answer "Nowhere." Others, "Everywhere." . . .

The second litmus test is a question rarely asked in social situations, but one I posed to every interviewee: *Where do you want to be buried?* A person with roots always knows the answer. . . . The response of a person without roots is quite different. "Wherever I am when I finish up," said one military brat. "I have no firm attachment to any geographic location." Another answered, "Buried? Never. I want to be cremated and my ashes scattered. I don't care where."[49]

I suppose there may be advantages to constant motion, though John Greenleaf Whittier didn't think so:

Yet, on life's current, he who drifts
  Is one with him who rows or rails;
And he who wanders widest lifts
  No more of beauty's jealous veils
Than he who from his doorway sees
  The miracle of flowers and trees.[50]

Military sociologists, after admitting the toll that father separation and nomadic living takes on children, do find one silver lining: "continuous relocations allowed them to have a broader perspective toward other peoples and races and thereby avoid the prejudicial stereotyping that was presumed or experienced among less mobile populations."[51] (One researcher claimed that among the manifold blessings of a childhood overseas was learning to answer "telephone calls in the foreign country.")[52]

Weigh these bagatelles against what Dr. Marc Fried found to be the common experience of families who move: "It is quite precise to speak of their reactions as expressions of grief . . . manifest in feelings of painful loss, the continued longing, the general depressive tone, frequent feelings of psychological or social or somatic distress . . . the sense of helplessness . . . anger . . . similar to mourning for a lost person."[53]

Children living on overseas bases have demonstrated "difficulty in making friends, a feeling of uninvolvement."[54] Families, as Eli M. Bower of the National Institute of Mental Health asserted thirty years ago, regard these foreign "communities as ephemeral stopovers. . . . Why be overly concerned about the crumbling walls, the unfixed walks, the burned-out bulbs, petty vandalism . . . in a home or community from which one may move next week, next month, or next year?"[55]

The military brat becomes inured to loss—hello and good-bye mean nothing. "People, you know, come and go," one daughter of a Marine sergeant told Mary Edwards Wertsch. "They can be jettisoned."[56] Or as an Air Force colonel's daughter said: "Everything was temporary when I was growing up. And that's the way I look at my life now: My job's only temporary. These clothes I'm wearing, this corporate image, is only temporary. My relationships are only going to be temporary."[57]

The average number of schools attended by those Wertsch interviewed was 9.5; these children are always the new kids, the kids not worth befriending because no sooner do you come to like them than off they go, into the wild blue yonder. Novelist Pat Conroy, author of *The Great Santini*, describes his brathood: "My job was to be a stranger, to know no one's name on the first day of school, to be ignorant of all history and flow and that familial sense of relationship and proportion that makes a town safe for a child. . . . *Home* is a foreign word in my vocabulary and always will be."[58]

At best, perpetual dislocation can breed a certain self-reliance. The son of an Air Force colonel replied, "Belonging? I suppose it means to feel comfortable with a set of people or a geographical location." Which he does not, so he chooses a different definition: "feeling you belong to yourself."[59]

This is all well and good if you've landed the starring role in an Ayn Rand novel, but the rest of us need anchorage. At least fatherless ghetto kids may form an attachment to a neighborhood; what of the military brats? (And remember, these children are the creation of government policy, not the free interplay of families and plane tickets.)

In 1944, as we were embarking on our national diaspora, James H. S. Bossard wrote that in adolescence

> we come to know, first and with the vivid freshness of youth, such community persons as the leading local educator, churchman, lawyer, civic leader, and banker. From knowing such persons, young people identify their ideals in terms of people, and vice versa. The adolescent who does not know his community and its leading personnel, who feels a sense of isolation in it, who has not taken and cannot take satisfactory root in it, is missing many of the indispensable requisites for normal, wholesome development.[60]

Yes, I know the extenuation: that somehow peeling potatoes in Iceland, or pressing buttons to annihilate Iraqi children is keeping America free, and so the missus and junior are the ultimate beneficiaries of dad's absence or life in a government housing project. We all kid ourselves, tell little fibs to get us through the day, and I am in no position to judge another man's balms.

But when discussing the dissolution of American family life and the devitalizing of local communities, let us at least not ignore the nine hundred-pound gorilla in the middle of the room. He is perhaps not as obvious as he was in 1944, but in a way he's more pervasive. Unlike in 1944, today's gorilla doesn't pretend he'll go away once the war's over. Because the war ain't ever gonna be over. The "peace dividend" that was to be rebated to American taxpayers after the Soviet Union's collapse vaporized; almost half a million of "the most virile of our men" are either at sea or overseas. More than one hundred thousand U.S. soldiers still occupy Germany alone.

War overturns the natural order of things—"In peace the sons bury their fathers, but in war the fathers bury their sons," according to Croesus—but even in peacetime, the maintenance of a large standing army is incompatible with American life as our forefathers and mothers understood it.

Is this really what we want?

NOTES

1. James Madison, *Notes of Debates in the Federal Convention of 1787 Reported by James Madison* (Athens: Ohio University Press, 1966/1840), p. 639.

2. Quoted in Arthur A. Ekirch, Jr., *The Civilian and the Military* (New York: Oxford University Press, 1956), p. 43.

3. Ibid., p. 3.

4. William H. Riker, *Soldiers of the States: The Role of the National Guard in American Democracy* (Washington, D.C.: Public Affairs Press, 1957), p. 12.

5. Ibid., p. 16.

6. Ibid., p. 50.

7. Quoted in Francis E. Merrill, "The Highway and Social Problems," in *Highways in Our National Life*, ed. Jean Labatut and Wheaton J. Lane (New York: Arno, 1972/1950), p. 137.

8. Ibid., p. 139.

9. John P. Marquand, *So Little Time* (Boston: Little, Brown, 1943), p. 93.

10. John W. Jeffries, *Wartime America: The World War II Home Front* (Chicago: Ivan R. Dee, 1996), p. 83.

11. Ibid., p. 83.

12. Richard Polenberg, ed., *America at War: The Home Front, 1941–1945* (Englewood Cliffs, NJ: Prentice-Hall, 1968), p. 126.

13. William M. Tuttle, Jr., *"Daddy's Gone to War": The Second World War in the Lives of America's Children* (New York: Oxford University Press, 1993), p. 31.

14. Josephine D. Abbott, "What of Youth in Wartime?" *Survey Midmonthly* 79 (October 1943): 265.

15. Jeffries, p. 89.

16. Quoted in C. Calvin Smith, *War and Wartime Changes: The Transformation of Arkansas 1940–1945* (Fayetteville: University of Arkansas Press, 1986), p. 48.

17. Quoted in Tuttle, p. 74.

18. Ellen Reese, "Maternalism and Political Mobilization: How California's Postwar Child Care Campaign Was Won," *Gender & Society* 10, no. 5 (October 1996): 574.

19. Ibid., p. 570.

20. Quoted in Richard Polenberg, *War and Society: The United States 1941–1945* (Philadelphia: J. B. Lippincott, 1972), p. 149.

21. Megan J. McClintock, "Civil War Pensions and the Reconstruction of Union Families," *Journal of American History* 83, no. 2 (September 1996): 458.

22. Ibid., p. 479.

23. Reuben Hill, *Families under Stress: Adjustment to the Crises of War Separation and Reunion* (New York: Harper & Brothers, 1949), pp. 52–53.

24. Ibid., p. 85.

25. Ibid., p. 126.

26. Quoted in Jeffries, p. 86.

27. Polenberg, p. 144.

28. Tuttle, p. 62.

29. Arch Merrill, *Slim Fingers Beckon* (New York: Stratford Press, 1951), p. 117.

30. *The Charter of the United Nations, Hearings before the Committee on Foreign Relations*, United States Senate, 79th Congress, 1st Session, p. 356.

31. Quoted in Tuttle, p. 260.

32. E. James Lieberman, "American Families and the Vietnam War," *Journal of Marriage and the Family* 33, no. 4 (November 1971): 715.

33. Ibid.

34. Nancy Shea, *The Army Wife* (New York: Harper & Brothers, 1941), p. xviii.

35. John Hess, *The Mobile Society: A History of the Moving and Storage Industry* (New York: McGraw-Hill, 1973), p. 74.

36. Ibid., p. 98.

37. William H. Whyte, Jr., *The Organization Man* (New York: Simon and Schuster, 1956), p. 276.

38. Ibid., p. 275.

39. Ellwyn R. Stoddard, "Changing Spouse Roles: An Analytical Commentary," in *Military Families: Adaptation to Change*, ed. Edna J. Hunter and Stephen Nice (New York: Praeger, 1978), pp. 161–62.

40. Mady Wechsler Segal, "Enlisted Family Life in the U.S. Army: A Portrait of a Community," in *Life in the Rank and File: Enlisted Men and Women in the Armed Forces of the United States, Australia, Canada, and the United Kingdom*, ed. David R. Segal and H. Wallace Sinaiko (Washington, D.C.: Pergamon-Brassey's, 1986), p. 191.

41. Frank A. Pedersen and Eugene J. Sullivan, "Relationships among Geographical Mobility, Parental Attitudes and Emotional Disturbances in Children," *American Journal of Orthopsychiatry* 34 (1964): 575.

42. Edna J. Hunter, *Families under the Flag* (New York: Praeger, 1982), p. 12.

43. Janice G. Rienerth, "Separation and Female-Centeredness in the Military Family," in *Military Families: Adaptation to Change*, pp. 172–173.

44. Hunter, p. 16.

45. Kathryn Brown Decker, "Coping with Sea Duty: Problems Encountered and Resources Utilized During Periods of Family Separation," in *Military Families: Adaptation to Change*, p. 119.

46. Hamilton I. McCubbin and Barbara B. Dahl, "Prolonged Family Separation in the Military: A Longitudinal Study," in *Families in the Military System*, ed. Hamilton I. McCubbin, Barbara B. Dahl, and Edna J. Hunter (Beverly Hills, Calif.: Sage, 1976), p. 115.

47. George E. Gardner, "Reactions of Children with Fathers and Brothers in the Armed Forces," *American Journal of Orthopsychiatry* 14 (1944): 38.

48. James H. S. Bossard, "Family Backgrounds of Wartime Adolescents," *The Annals of the American Academy of Political and Social Science* 236 (November 1944): 40.

49. Mary Edwards Wertsch, Military Brats: Legacies of Childhood Inside the Fortress (New York: Harmony, 1991), pp. 249–50.

50. John Greenleaf Whittier, "The Last Walk in Autumn," *Snowbound, Among the Hills, Songs of Labor and Other Poems* (Boston: Houghton Mifflin, 1916), p. 85.

51. Paul Darnauer, "The Adolescent Experience in Career Army Families," in *Families in the Military System*, p. 64.

52. Hunter, p. 39.

53. Quoted in Jerry L. McKain, "Alienation: A Function of Geographic Mobility among Families," in *Families in the Military System*, p. 69.

54. Hamilton I. McCubbin, Barbara B. Dahl, and Edna J. Hunter, "Research on the Military Family: A Review," in *Families in the Military System*, p. 326.

55. Eli M. Bower, "American Children and Families in Overseas Communities," *American Journal of Orthopsychiatry* 37, no. 4 (1967): 791.

56. Quoted in Wertsch, p. 269.

57. Ibid., p. 275.

58. Ibid., p. xviii.

59. Ibid., pp. 421–22.

60. Bossard, p. 41.

Bibliographical Note

The endnotes contain my sources; the interpretations thereof, for better or worse, are mine. In particular I commend the following writings:

CHAPTER ONE

Charlotte Perkins Gilman's *The Home: Its Work and Influence* (New York: McClure, Phillips, & Co., 1903) is an honest and terrifying call to dissever work—indeed, the family itself—from the home. Stranger-provided day care, communal eateries, the home reduced to a TV-blaring pit stop for dual-earner couples—Gilman saw it coming. That she applauded it makes her no less prescient.

CHAPTER TWO

Wayne E. Fuller's *The Old Country School* (Chicago: University of Chicago, 1982) is simply splendid. The essays of Wendell Berry—for instance "The Work of Local Culture" in *What Are People For?* (San Francisco: North Point, 1990)—are indispensable. His life and work are patriotism made flesh and word. Thomas J. Fleming's "Egalitarianism, Centralization, and the Debasement of American Education," *Essays in Political Economy* (Ludwig von Mises Institute, July 1991), is typically trenchant. For more on the merits of small-scale education, see Kirkpatrick Sale's *Human Scale* (New York: Coward, McCann & Geoghegan, 1980) and Deborah Meier's *The Power of Their Ideas* (Boston: Beacon, 1995).

CHAPTER THREE

The handful of works on the antisuffragists are almost uniformly (and drearily) hostile. A shining exception is Manuela Thurner's "Better Citizens without the Ballot," included in *One Woman, One Vote*, edited by Marjorie Spruill Wheeler (Troutdale, Oreg.: NewSage Press, 1995). An earlier version of Thurner's essay appeared in the *Journal of Women's History* 5, no. 1 (Spring 1993). The keenest of the traditionalist Antis, Ruth Whitney Lyman, contributed to the joltingly uneven *Anti-Suffrage Essays by Massachusetts Women* (Boston: Forum, 1916). Christopher Lasch, in "Life in the Therapeutic State," from the posthumously published *Women and the Common Life* (New York: Norton, 1997), sees suffrage as "an integral part" of a progressive movement that sought "to deflect Populism, labor radicalism, and other potentially revolutionary movements by reforming society from the top down."

CHAPTER FOUR

The standard work is Paul K. Conkin's *Tomorrow a New World* (Ithaca, N.Y.: Cornell University Press, 1959). Professor Conkin is rather more admiring of the New Deal than I am. Fathers Luigi G. Ligutti and John C. Rawe, authors of *Rural Roads to Security* (Milwaukee: Bruce, 1940), were heroic men of the cloth but, alas, prosaic men of the pen.

CHAPTER FIVE

Andrew Lytle's "The Hind Tit" contains a devastating account of the changes wreaked—and culture wrecked—by "good roads." The essay is a standout in the classic agrarian volume *I'll Take My Stand* (New York: Harper Bros., 1930; reprinted Baton Rouge: Louisiana State University Press, 1977). One sociologist who saw early on just how wide a swath the highways were cutting was Francis E. Merrill; see "The Highway and Social Problems," in *Highways in Our National Life*, edited by Jean Labatut and Wheaton J. Lane (New York: Arno, 1972/1950).

CHAPTER SIX

The military's role in undermining American family life has gone unexamined these many years, perhaps because the conservatives who claim to cherish family life are all too often unblinking and unthinking defenders of the American Empire. The exception to this rule has been Allan Carlson; see " 'You're in the Army Now': The Troubled State of the Military Family," *The Family in America* 3, no. 11 (November 1989). The cost of empire has been measured—brilliantly, wittily, mournfully—in novels and essays by the great American man of letters Gore Vidal. Feast upon his *United States: Essays 1952–1992* (New York: Random House, 1993).

Index

About the Author

BILL KAUFFMAN is a contributing editor to *Chronicles* and *Liberty*. His work has appeared in *The Nation*, *The Los Angeles Times Book Review*, and *The Wall Street Journal*. He is the author of three books: *America First! Its History, Culture, and Politics* (1995), *Country Towns of New York* (1994), and *Every Man a King* (1989). He lives with his wife and daughter in his native Genesee County, New York.